D0077989

African Arguments

African Arguments is a series of short books about Africa today. Aimed at the growing number of students and general readers who want to know more about the continent, these books highlight many of the longer-term strategic as well as immediate political issues. They will get to the heart of why Africa is the way it is and how it is changing. The books are scholarly but engaged, substantive as well as topical.

Titles already published

Alex de Waal, *AIDS and Power: Why There is No Political Crisis – Yet*

Raymond W. Copson, *The United States in Africa: Bush Policy and Beyond*

Chris Alden, *China in Africa*

Tom Porteous, *Britain in Africa*

Julie Flint and Alex de Waal, *Darfur: A New History of a Long War*, revised and updated edition

Jonathan Glennie, *The Trouble with Aid: Why Less Could Mean More for Africa*

Peter Uvin, *Life after Violence: A People's Story of Burundi*

Bronwen Manby, *Struggles for Citizenship in Africa*

Camilla Toulmin, *Climate Change in Africa*

Orla Ryan, *Chocolate Nations: Living and Dying for Chocolate in West Africa*

Theodore Trefon, *Congo Masquerade: The Political Culture of Aid Inefficiency and Reform Failure*

Léonce Ndikumana and James Boyce, *Africa's Odious Debts: How Foreign Loans and Capital Flight Bled a Continent*

Mary Harper, *Getting Somalia Wrong? Faith, War and Hope in a Shattered State*

Forthcoming

Gerard McCann, *India and Africa – Old Friends, New Game*

Gernot Klantschnig and Neil Carrier, *Africa and the War on Drugs: Narcotics in Sub-Saharan Africa*

Tim Allen, *Trial Justice: The Lord's Resistance Army, Sudan and the International Criminal Court*, revised and updated edition

Published by Zed Books with the support of the following organizations:

International African Institute The International African Institute's principal aim is to promote scholarly understanding of Africa, notably its changing societies, cultures and languages. Founded in 1926 and based in London, it supports a range of seminars and publications including the journal *Africa*. <www.internationalafricaninstitute.org>

Royal African Society Now more than a hundred years old, the Royal African Society today is Britain's leading organization promoting Africa's cause. Through its journal, *African Affairs*, and by organizing meetings, discussions and other activities, the society strengthens links between Africa and Britain and encourages understanding of Africa and its relations with the rest of the world. <www.royalafrican society.org>

Social Science Research Council The Social Science Research Council brings much-needed expert knowledge to public issues. Founded in 1923 and based in New York, it brings together researchers, practitioners and policy-makers in every continent. <www.ssrc.org>

About the author

Mary Harper is a BBC journalist special-
izing in Africa. She has reported from
Somalia since the outbreak of civil war
in 1991 and from other conflict zones in
Africa. She has written for several publications, including the *Economist*, *The Times*
and the *Washington Post*. She has degrees
from Cambridge University and the School
of Oriental and African Studies in London.

GETTING SOMALIA WRONG?

FAITH, WAR AND HOPE IN A SHATTERED STATE

Mary Harper

Zed Books
LONDON | NEW YORK

in association with

International African Institute
Royal African Society
Social Science Research Council

Getting Somalia wrong? Faith, war and hope in a shattered state was first published in association with the International African Institute, the Royal African Society and the Social Science Research Council in 2012 by Zed Books Ltd, 7 Cynthia Street, London N1 9JF, UK and Room 400, 175 Fifth Avenue, New York, NY 10010, USA

www.zedbooks.co.uk
www.internationalafricaninstitute.org
www.royalafricansociety.org
www.ssrc.org

Set in Monotype Plantin and FontFont Kievit by Ewan Smith, London
Index: ed.emery@thefreeuniversity.net
Cover designed by Rogue Four Design
Printed and bound by the CPI Group (UK) Ltd, Croydon CR0 4YY

Distributed in the USA exclusively by Palgrave Macmillan, a division of St Martin's Press, LLC, 175 Fifth Avenue, New York, NY 10010, USA

A catalogue record for this book is available from the British Library
Library of Congress Cataloging in Publication Data available

ISBN 978 1 84277 932 3 hb
ISBN 978 1 84277 933 0 pb

CONTENTS

Illustrations | viii Acknowledgements | ix
Author's note | x Chronology | xi
Glossary | xiv

Introduction 1

1 Clan and country 14

2 History 44

3 Islamism 71

4 A failed state? 105

5 Piracy 142

6 Somalia and the outside world . . 166

Conclusion 197

Notes | 202 Bibliography | 208
Index | 210

ILLUSTRATIONS

Maps

1.1 Somalia 15

1.2 'Greater Somalia' and geographical distribution of
major clans 32

1.3 Main sub-divisions of Somali territory 35

4.1 Reach of Somali pirate attacks, 2005–10 144

Figure

1.1 Somali clan families 37

Photographs

1 Displaced woman and child in Mogadishu famine zone,
August 2011 2

2 Women soldiers in the transitional government army . 25

3 Displaced boy in Mogadishu plays with a gun made
from a stick 68

4 Al-Shabaab fighters in Mogadishu 75

5 Mogadishu after the withdrawal of al-Shabaab,
September 2011 87

6 'Pavement banker' in Hargeisa 122

7 Women police officers in Somaliland 138

8 Somali pirate, Ismail Elixh 151

9 An al-Shabaab fighter distributes food parcels in Lower
Shabelle famine zone, September 2011 182

10 Displaced people queue for food rations in
Mogadishu 185

11 Somali trader in an Eastleigh shopping mall 195

ACKNOWLEDGEMENTS

This book is in many ways the combined efforts of several people. Mohamed Adde of the BBC Somali service gave generously of his time, his knowledge and his contacts; I could not have written this book without him. The same can be said for my colleague, Mohamed Moalimuu, in Mogadishu. Stephanie Kitchen believed in me from the start, and gave me constant reassurance and encouragement. Thank you too to my other editors, Ken Barlow, Alex de Waal, Richard Dowden and Robert Molteno. My colleagues and friends at the BBC Somali service, past and present, have taught me so much. They are too many to list individually, but I would like to give special mention to Ahmed Said Egeh, Abdullahi Haji, Yusuf Hassan, Bashkas Jugsodaay, Yonis Nur, Yusuf Garaad Omar, Abdirazak Haji Mohamed Sirad and Hussein Aw Jama Jibril Xagar. I would also like to thank Mohammed Adow, Abdirashid Duale, Abdulkader Hashi Elmi, Abdullah Farah, Julie Flint, Sally Healy, Ian Hoare, Karen O'Brien and James Wylie. My greatest thanks are to my family. To my mother, Gay Harper, for introducing me to Somalia in the first place when she worked as a nurse in Mogadishu during the worst of the fighting in the early 1990s. To my father, Malcolm Harper, who is a constant inspiration, if exacting taskmaster. To my brother and sisters, and most of all to my children, Johnny and Antonia, who have had to put up for far too long with a mother distracted with matters Somali.

AUTHOR'S NOTE

As a journalist who has followed events in Somalia for the past two decades, I have had the privilege of meeting and learning from people at every level of Somali society, from presidents to pirates, from millionaire businessmen to those who have lost everything. It would have been impossible for me to do my work without these people, some of whom have put their lives or livelihoods at risk by speaking to me. I rely for much of my work on the brave Somali journalists, who live in dangerous places and speak to me almost daily about what is happening. From time to time, they call me in great excitement to tell me there has been no fighting that day, something so unusual that, for them, it is 'news'. Some of these journalists have been forced into exile; others have lost their lives.

The information in this book comes from what I have seen in Somalia and the diaspora, what I have heard from Somalis and those interested in the country, and what I have read about it. Although I refer to academic texts, this book is much less a work of scholarship than an attempt to present a picture, or series of pictures, of the situation, in the hope that it might improve understanding. My research has been severely restricted by the conflict, and what I have to say is inevitably incomplete. There are many other stories to tell, and many other arguments to present.

CHRONOLOGY

7–10th centuries AD   Arab and Persian traders settle in port towns along the coast, spreading Islam.

17th century   Period of Omani influence along southern Somali coast.

1875   Egypt occupies some coastal towns and parts of Somali interior.

1897   Imperial partition of Somalia. Britain, Ethiopia, France and Italy divide the region up among themselves.

1900–20   The 'Mad Mullah' Seyyid Mohamed Abdulle Hassan's jihad against Somalia's colonizers, especially Britain and Ethiopia.

1934   Italy goes to war with Ethiopia.

1940   Italy occupies British Protectorate of Somaliland.

1941   Allies defeat Italy. British Military Administration established throughout the Somali region, except French Somaliland.

1943   Foundation of Somalia's first major nationalist party, the Somali Youth League.

1946   'Bevin Plan'. British foreign minister Ernest Bevin proposes the unification of all Somali regions. This is rejected.

1950   *Somalia Italiana* placed under UN trusteeship, to be administered by Italy with a ten-year mandate. British Somaliland reverts to former protectorate status. The Ogaden is returned to Ethiopia.

26 June 1960   Independence of British Somaliland.

1 July 1960   *Somalia Italiana* becomes independent and joins Somaliland to form the Republic of Somalia.

1963   Insurrection in the Ogaden leads to a brief outbreak of fighting between Somalia and Ethiopia.

1963–67   Somali *shifta* campaign for Somali independence from Kenya in the north-eastern region.

21 October 1969   Civilian government overthrown in a military coup led by General Mohamed Siad Barre. 'Scientific socialism' introduced with help from the Soviet Union.

1973–74   National literacy campaign, introducing written Somali.

1974–75   Devastating drought and famine lead to massive displacement of northern nomads to agricultural and fishing collectives in southern Somalia.

1977   French Somaliland becomes the independent Republic of Djibouti under ethnic Somali president Hassan Guled Aptidon. Ogaden nationalist rebellion in Ethiopia.

1977–78   Ethiopian–Somali war. Somalia is defeated after the Soviet Union changes sides. Abortive coup against Siad Barre.

1982   Formation of north-eastern rebel group, Somali Salvation Democratic Front, and north-western Somali Nation Movement. Both are based in Ethiopia.

1988   Opposition United Somali Congress founded in Rome.

26 January 1991   President Siad Barre overthrown by USC. Faction fighting erupts in Mogadishu and elsewhere in Somalia.

18 May 1991   SNM declares independence of Somaliland.

1992–93   United Nations Operation Restore Hope; 30,000 US and other troops launch peacekeeping operation.

May 1993   Operation Restore Hope hands over to UNOSOM II.

5 June 1993   Faction leader Mohamed Farah Aideed's forces kill more than twenty Pakistani peacekeepers in Mogadishu.

October 1993   Black Hawk Down incident in Mogadishu. Hundreds of Somalis and eighteen US troops killed.

1994   US troops withdraw from Somalia.

1995   UN peacekeepers leave Somalia.

1998 North-eastern region of Puntland declares autonomy.

2000 Arta peace conference held in Djibouti. Abdulqasim Salad Hassan elected by delegates as transitional national president.

2002–04 Mbagathi peace conference in Kenya elects Abdullahi Yusuf as president of transitional federal government.

2006 Union of Islamic Courts takes power in much of south-central Somalia.

December 2006 Ethiopian invasion. UIC overthrown.

2007 Transitional federal government moves to Mogadishu. African Union peacekeepers deployed.

2008 NATO agrees to dispatch a naval force to waters off Somalia in an effort to control piracy.

2009 Ethiopian troops withdraw from Somalia. Former UIC leader Sheikh Sharif Sheikh Ahmed elected transitional president at Djibouti peace conference.

2010 Islamist al-Shabaab movement, which controls much of south-central Somalia, publicly declares allegiance to al-Qaeda.

11 July 2010 Seventy-four people killed as they watch football World Cup final in Kampala, Uganda. Al-Shabaab says it carried out the suicide attacks.

July 2011 United Nations declares famine in parts of south-central Somalia.

October 2011 Kenya launches military incursion into southern Somalia aimed at clearing al-Shabaab from the region.

GLOSSARY

adoon	slave
Ahlu Sunna Wa Jamaa	Somali Sufi group
al-Itihaad al-Islamiya	Somali Islamist group
al-Shabaab	Somali Islamist group
AMISOM	African Union peacekeeping force
ARPCT	Alliance for the Restoration of Peace and Counter-Terrorism
AU	African Union
barkin	wooden headrest
Benadiri	Arab communities living in coastal areas
diya	blood money
guurti	assembly of elders
haj	pilgrimage to Mecca
hawala	informal money transfer system
Hizbul Islam	Somali Islamist group
IGAD	Intergovernmental Authority on Development
Jareer	descendants of slaves and settled farmers, Bantus
qat	narcotic leaf
shir	assembly of elders
SNM	Somali National Movement
SSDF	Somali Salvation Democratic Front
TFG	transitional federal government
TNG	transitional national government
UIC	Union of Islamic Courts
UNOSOM	United Nations peacekeeping force in Somalia
USC	United Somali Congress
xawilaad	informal money transfer system
xeer	customary law

INTRODUCTION

Somalia has one of the worst reputations in the world. It is frequently referred to as the epitome of a 'failed state'[1] and has been described by the United States and others as a haven for al-Qaeda. Aid agencies have said Somalia suffers from 'the world's worst humanitarian crisis';[2] other groups class it as the 'most corrupt'.[3] Somalia even suffers the ignominy of having 'the dodgiest passports in the world'.[4]

Media reports talk of a country surrounded by 'pirate-infested waters'[5] and of the capital, Mogadishu, as 'the most dangerous place in the world'.[6] The word 'Mogadishu' has entered some people's vocabulary as a way of describing a place or situation that is truly terrible. *Mogadishu* was the title of a British play which premiered in 2011; it was not about Somalia, but a troubled inner-city secondary school in England. While covering the riots that hit some parts of England in August 2011, a BBC reporter described the Tottenham district of London as looking like Mogadishu.

I asked a group of British children what they knew about Somalia. A teenage boy mimed the action of a machine gun spraying bullets. He said his schoolmates were scared of what he called the 'Malis' because they 'stuck together in a gang'. 'Your life would be finished if you did anything to a "Mali",' he said. A nine-year-old boy said Somalia was a place where 'people are poor and have lots of guns'. A girl told me Somalia was full of pirates, another said there were child soldiers.

Somalia ticks all the boxes for an African disaster zone. It has war, it has hunger. It provides perfect images for the media:

1 Displaced woman and child in Mogadishu famine zone, August 2011 (Mohamed Moalimuu)

gun-wielding, drug-crazed teenagers race around in sawn-off Land Cruisers, while skeletal women clutch starving children, flies buzzing around their faces. Such pictures were available in abundance in July 2011, when Somalia leapt back onto the world's television screens following the declaration by the United Nations of a famine in some parts of the country.

These images and labels act as barriers to other ways of seeing Somalia. More than two decades of conflict and crisis have forced Somalis to invent alternative political and economic systems. They have enthusiastically seized modern technology, fusing it with pre-colonial traditions to create some of the most advanced and effective money transfer systems on the continent and one of the cheapest, most developed mobile phone networks in East Africa.

This book argues that there is a lot to be learned from the Somali way of doing things, and that there is more to the country than violence, hunger, piracy and Islamist extremism. It will also explain how it came about that, for more than twenty years,

Somalia has had no functioning central authority. The book will examine the role of foreign powers and international organizations, and ask whether responses to Somalia, particularly from the United States and its allies, have helped the country or, as a growing number of experts have argued, have contributed towards its destruction as a viable nation-state.

Although many things work in Somalia, albeit often in unusual ways, the scale of its problems should not be underestimated. Since the collapse of national government in 1991 and the ensuing years of conflict, it has ceased to exist as a coherent political entity. The country has splintered into a patchwork of semi-autonomous regions whose boundaries shift constantly. Some of these areas are relatively stable, especially the self-declared republic of Somaliland, which is not recognized internationally but has a relatively democratic government, a developing economy and several other features of a fully functioning society. The issue of Somaliland is highly contentious; although it operates to all intents and purposes as an independent polity, it is considered by the Somali transitional government and internationally as officially part of Somalia as a whole. When relevant, I will distinguish between the two territories by referring to them as 'Somalia' and 'Somaliland'; at other times, particularly when describing events prior to 1991, the terms 'Somalia' and 'Somali' will encompass both areas.

By 2011, many Somalis, aid workers, diplomats, academics and others had mentally divided the territory into three, referring to it as the separate units of 'south-central', Puntland and Somaliland, even if they officially recognized it as a single country.

Most other regions of Somalia do not fit into any familiar paradigm of statehood; they do not work according to principles that can be easily understood by the outside world. They are often violent and unpredictable, with power changing hands at a rapid rate. This situation is considered by many to be a threat to the Somalis themselves, to their neighbours and to the wider world.

Somalia is frequently referred to as a 'failed state', suggesting that nothing works in the country and that there is no security or development. When considering the value of this label, it is important to bear in mind the conditions in Somalia before the collapse of functioning central government. There were always centrifugal forces at work; the country was in a perpetual state of potential disintegration, even when it was governed by the ruthless dictator Siad Barre from 1969 to 1991. Siad Barre's attempts to impose a centralized authoritarian government, and the development of a personality cult around him, ultimately led to his downfall; a destructive war with Ethiopia in the 1970s and the alienation of powerful Somali clans and other interest groups meant that his grip on power had started to slip years before he was ousted in January 1991.

It would therefore be misleading to describe Somalia as ever having been a stable, fully functioning nation-state, democratic or otherwise. A new model of statehood needs to be developed for Somalia, perhaps one that combines modern and traditional types of governance, and also one that gives a degree of autonomy to the different regions.

The bewildering recent history of the country, coupled with its chronic disorder, have led to serious misunderstandings in international policy, with damaging consequences for Somalia, the Horn of Africa and beyond. The misconceptions became especially acute in 2006 when an alliance of sharia courts, known as the Union of Islamic Courts (UIC), took control of large parts of the country until it was dislodged by US-backed Ethiopian invaders supporting the forces of a weak transitional government.

The USA and its allies misinterpreted these events. They mistakenly equated a home-grown form of political Islam with the international al-Qaeda franchise and, by doing so, inadvertently advertised the country as a promising new battle front for jihadists from across the world. In its original form, the UIC did not represent a new front for violent Islamism; sharia courts had for several years been providing order and justice in some parts of Somalia where authority had collapsed. They carried out harsh punishments such as amputations, but they also provided safety for the majority. People could walk in the streets of Mogadishu without fear for the first time since the eruption of civil conflict.

However, the worst fears of the USA and others have now come true. After the UIC was driven out in 2007, elements of the movement re-emerged as the violent Islamist al-Shabaab militia, which does represent a threat to the outside world. Foreign fighters have joined Somali Islamists, and, in February 2010, al-Shabaab for the first time publicly linked itself with al-Qaeda.

Because it is viewed as a haven for al-Qaeda and its allies, Somalia has been squeezed into the dominant Western post-9/11 narrative. It has become the 'African Iraq', the 'African Afghanistan'. And like Iraq and Afghanistan, Somalia represents an interesting case study for analysing the successes and failures of US-led foreign policy.

Kenya made ample use of 'War on Terror' rhetoric in October 2011 when, for the first time since independence, it launched a military offensive in a foreign state. Its troops invaded southern Somalia with the aim of eliminating al-Shabaab, whose presence along the Kenyan border and in refugee camps within Kenya itself, posed a serious security threat. The Kenyan military was supported from the air by American drones, which took off from bases in Ethiopia and launched numerous attacks on suspected al-Shabaab targets.

Much of the international reaction to Somalia suggests a failure to appreciate that the country will not submit passively to meddling and experimentation. Somalia should not simply be seen as an unwitting chess piece in the 'War on Terror'. Somalis have their own identity and history, and a powerful will. Some in Somalia know how to take advantage of the country being labelled as a 'failed state' and a breeding ground for terrorists. Politicians and warlords have craftily accused their political adversaries of Islamist extremism in order to gain foreign financial and military support.

Somalia has always been difficult for outsiders to deal with and to understand. The dominant global image of the country is vividly conveyed in the Hollywood movie *Black Hawk Down*. The film tells how, in October 1993, militias loyal to the warlord Mohamed Farah Aideed killed eighteen US servicemen in Mogadishu after shooting down two American Black Hawk helicopters. The incident had a traumatic impact on Americans, who saw on their television screens the naked bodies of US soldiers being dragged through the streets by crowds of jeering Somalis. What had started as a mercy mission to feed starving Africans became a humiliating disaster for the USA. Within months of the incident, American troops had withdrawn from Somalia, to be replaced by an equally unsuccessful United Nations force, which itself soon left the country, leading to years of international neglect. Somalia was largely left to its own devices, and, as the world turned its back on the territory, fishermen turned into pirates and moderate Islamists became al-Qaeda-linked militants.

The predominant Western reaction to the 'Black Hawk Down' incident was one of hurt amazement: how could an impoverished nation of nomads force the most powerful country on earth to abandon what was originally intended as a humanitarian intervention? But this was not the first time Somalia had stood up to the world's great powers.

Although not as well known as the story of the 'Great Game' in Afghanistan, when for 100 years the Russian and British empires tried and failed to subdue the territory, the modern history of Somalia is one of a proud people resisting and outwitting the strongest forces of the day. Since the early days of European contact with Africa, Somalis have captured the imagination of writers and thinkers. The explorer Richard Burton described them as a 'fierce and turbulent race of republicans';[7] the social anthropologist Professor Ioan Lewis, probably the most prolific and significant academic authority on Somalia, writes that they have 'an open contempt for other people'.[8]

An earlier counterpart to 'Black Hawk Down' is the story of the 'Mad Mullah'. Given this nickname by his British enemies, Seyyid Mohamed Abdulle Hassan was a warrior poet who battled against colonial forces for the first two decades of the twentieth century. He led what he described as a jihad or holy war against the infidel. Like the Somalis of today, he fought to keep the region free from European, Ethiopian and Christian influences. He held them back for several years, but Somali-dominated territories were ultimately divided up and ruled or colonized by Ethiopia, Britain, Italy and France. James Rennell Rodd, who led the British mission in Somalia, could have been writing about the present day when he said 'many valuable lives were lost and millions spent in thankless expeditions against the elusive enemy who gave us so much trouble over a period of twenty years'.[9]

The 'Mad Mullah' used words as well as force; his poetry motivated his supporters, and, to this day, he remains an inspiration. Somalis continue to quote his poems with pride and passion, not in remembrance of the battles against the British, but transposed to the country's current relationship with the USA and its allies. Somalia retains an oral culture, with poetry and songs featuring prominently in daily life; many use poems and proverbs to help them illustrate, discuss and resolve a wide range of problems.

Throughout history, most efforts by foreign nations to intervene in Somalia have backfired. Fundamental misunderstandings about the country mean that even when the outside world appears genuinely to want to provide help in a humanitarian disaster, as in the early 1990s when the civil war and harsh environmental circumstances led to famine, it can end up contributing to further collapse and disintegration, provoking conflict when it means to promote peace.

Most outside efforts to encourage Somalis to solve their own problems have also ended in failure. By 2007, there had been no fewer than fourteen national reconciliation conferences aimed at ending the numerous conflicts that arose after the fall of Siad Barre. These huge and expensive gatherings are usually funded by foreign countries and international organizations and often held outside Somalia. They sometimes drag on for years and have had little lasting impact on life inside the country. Since the 1990s, many Somali leaders have spent far more time discussing how to restore order than doing anything practical to improve the lives of ordinary people. It is surprising that foreign powers are still prepared to pay for these meetings. The fact that Somalis are still able to persuade outsiders to fund their national reconciliation conferences is an example of how good some of them are at exploiting their situation. They have had years to develop skills in extracting valuable resources from foreigners, especially when it comes to emergency assistance or support for peace-building. Twenty years of talking about peace, often in hotels or other comfortable settings outside Somalia, have contributed to a great divide between the Somali leadership and the people left behind to endure the continuing conflict and uncertainty.

It is precisely because their leaders and the world at large have failed to restore stability that Somalis have created their own survival mechanisms. The perspective of the country as a 'failed state' is dangerously limiting; in spite of the apparent chaos and lack of central authority, there are aspects of society that have continued to function effectively, even in the regions most badly affected by conflict. Some, such as trade and communications, have thrived, particularly in the money transfer, mobile phone and livestock sectors. An analysis that focuses too closely on the absence of central government may overlook the potential value of social, political and economic mechanisms that are peculiar to Somalia but may provide useful models for other countries affected by conflict and state collapse.

By viewing the whole country through the lens of the capital, Mogadishu, many descriptions of Somalia project an image of a nation in a permanent state of war with itself. However, large areas are quite peaceful, with their own administrations, legal systems and economies. The situation in the self-declared republic of Somaliland has been so buoyant that many refugees who fled the terrible civil war of the late 1980s have returned home. Another area of relative stability is the neighbouring north-eastern region of Puntland, which has set up its own semi-autonomous administration, although it was for some time a major pirate stronghold.

It is ironic that the explosion of violence in central and southern Somalia in 2007 resulted from an international intervention to oust an organization that had, for the first time since the early 1990s, managed to establish a degree of stability. One reason why the Union of Islamic Courts was successful in its attempt to restore order was because, to a large extent, it evolved from the bottom up. Like Hamas in the Palestinian territories and, to a lesser extent, the Muslim Brotherhood in Egypt, the sharia courts gained support because they provided essential services to a neglected population. Filling a vacuum, the courts started to perform some of the key functions of government in a stateless society. It was probably not the Islamic nature of the authority that was of primary importance to the community it served; it was the fact that, for the brief six months the courts were in power, life was safer than it had been for many years. This is in some ways similar to the situation in Afghanistan during Taliban rule, where, although little was provided in the way of social services, there was finally a degree of law and order after many years of violent chaos.

The population paid a price for peace and continue to do

so in the many parts of Somalia controlled by militant Islamist groups, which have become far more extreme than the UIC. Bloody sharia punishments, including public executions, have been carried out; the popular stimulant *qat*, so integral to Somali culture, has been banned; women have to cover themselves with thick, dark robes; and people are forbidden from watching films and football matches in public video parlours.

Even when there is no semblance of civil order, some aspects of the economy and society have flourished. Somalia is one of the most conflict-ridden countries in Africa, but it was one of the first to develop a mobile phone system. As it collapsed into civil war, it became one of the easiest African countries to communicate with, simply bypassing the era of the crackling, unreliable landline.

Internet use is another modern phenomenon that has developed rapidly among Somali communities around the world. The need for information and their desire to speak, trade and interact with each other know no boundaries. Somalis love to gossip, especially about politics, and the huge diaspora, stretching from America to Australia, from the Gulf to Scandinavia, buzzes enthusiastically in cyberspace. These sophisticated and almost exclusively Somali lines of communication are essential for the maintenance of their complicated trading links across the world. Somalis transport and sell their livestock deep into Kenya and across the Red Sea to the Gulf states. The stimulant leaf, *qat*, is flown from Ethiopia and Kenya, not only to Somalia but also to other parts of the world inhabited by Somalis.

It is in some ways surprising that Somalia is so dysfunctional as a modern 'nation-state'. Unlike most other African countries, it is not torn apart by tribalism. It is almost unique in sub-Saharan Africa in that the vast majority of its population shares the same language, ethnicity, culture and religion. It is ironic that the main other example of such a homogenous African country is Botswana, one of the continent's most successful states.

The unity in Somalia is, however, counteracted by the clan system, which is inherently divisive. The clan has an almost end-lessly splitting structure and poses serious obstacles to attempts to impose central authority. At the time of writing, the transitional government operated on the principle of there being four main clans in the country, although many dispute this. Clans divide into sub-clans, which divide again and again, sometimes ending up as a group of just a few families, which identifies itself as a separate clan with its own distinct name. This popular Somali proverb illustrates the divisive nature of the society:

Me and my clan against the world;
Me and my family against my clan;
Me and my brother against my family;
Me against my brother.[10]

Clans are confusing, even to Somalis themselves, some of whom deny the significance of their role and are reluctant to disclose to which group they belong. What is clear is that whatever political system is introduced is almost immediately transformed by the clan, which is stronger and more durable than any form of government. The clan, however, is not a stable entity; it is dynamic, infinitely adaptable and constantly being remoulded by the political situation in the country.

The clan becomes most important in times of conflict; many urban Somalis say they had no idea to which clan their friends and neighbours belonged until the start of the civil war. As warring factions often develop in line with the clans, Somalis have little choice but to identify with their clan when conflict breaks out. The rise of Islamist groups has gone some way towards diluting the importance of the clan, but it is far from certain whether it will permanently erode clan identity.

Siad Barre believed that the only way to govern effectively was to eliminate clan politics. After taking power by force in

October 1969, he attempted to break clanism by imposing a form of socialism. By introducing a written form of the Somali language in the 1970s, and vigorously supporting a nationwide literacy programme, he attempted to instil a sense of national identity. But Siad Barre's dictatorship was a thinly disguised form of domination by his own Darod clan, and clan politics proved his eventual undoing. It was the intense hatred of the Darod by clans that considered themselves the rightful inhabitants of Mogadishu which led to the uprising that eventually saw the defeat of Siad Barre, and his flight from the capital in January 1991. Further proof of the inherent instability of Somalia under the Siad Barre dictatorship came just five months later when the north of the country broke away, declaring itself the independent republic of Somaliland. Its borders, to a large degree, mirrored those of the British protectorate, also known as 'Somaliland', which was separate from the Italian colony to the south, known as 'Somalia' and governed in a very different way.

Another factor that works against Somalia's viability as a stable nation-state is the fact that its ethnic, linguistic and cultural coherence extends far beyond its territorial boundaries. The five-pointed white star on the light blue Somali flag represents 'Greater Somalia', a vast area encompassing the Somali-speaking regions of Ethiopia, Djibouti and northern Kenya as well as Somaliland and Somalia. This creates problems, not only for Somalia, but for its immediate neighbours, all of which have large and restive ethnic Somali populations. Trouble in Somalia can mean trouble across the Horn of Africa.

There are many fundamental differences between the way Somalia works and common characteristics of the contemporary nation-state. Outsiders tend to find it a hard place to understand, and there is generally a wide gap between the various attempts made to introduce solutions to its problems and the reality lived by its population. The best people to sort out the problem of

Somalia are the Somalis themselves, and this has already been proved to some degree in the self-declared republic of Somaliland. It is ironic that the region that was largely left alone by foreign powers, and received very little outside help, is one of the most stable, and certainly the most democratic, of all territories in the Horn of Africa. Lessons can be drawn from the Somaliland experience, although they cannot be applied directly to the rest of Somalia, which has over the past two decades followed a very different path. Foreign powers have a role to play in Somalia, particularly because the existence of al-Qaeda-linked groups and piracy have an international impact. But until Somalia is more clearly understood and a different approach is found, it will continue to perplex, alarm and threaten the outside world, and it will be very difficult to find a way forward for the country which works for both Somalis and non-Somalis alike.

1 | CLAN AND COUNTRY

Although it is part of the African continent, Somalia points outwards and upwards towards the Arab world (see Map 1.1). Its shape resembles the horn of a rhinoceros; it is sharp and aggressive, forming the outer part of the Horn of Africa. The country's proximity to the Arabian Peninsula, together with its 3,000-kilometre coastline facing east towards the Indian Ocean and north to the strategic Gulf of Aden, means that for centuries Somalis have seen themselves as part of a world beyond Africa.

Somalis are an outward-looking, travelling people, despite the fact that their society is relatively closed. They have a strong seafaring tradition, and for many years provided large numbers of crew for international ocean-going vessels. Perhaps this, together with their strategically situated coastline, which is the longest in Africa, helps explain why they are so well placed to have become the world's most active twenty-first-century pirates, who, by the late 2000s, were seizing dozens of ships and hundreds of hostages every year.

It is not only Somalia's geography which points it away from Africa. There is of course great diversity within the continent, but the differences between Somalis and most other Africans are especially acute. This makes it difficult, even impossible, to apply to Somalia most models, theories or 'ways of thinking' about sub-Saharan Africa. Many Somalis do not see themselves as African; they are somehow apart, and often make cruel jokes at the expense of people they describe as 'Africans', 'blacks' or 'those with broad noses'. One reason for this sense of otherness

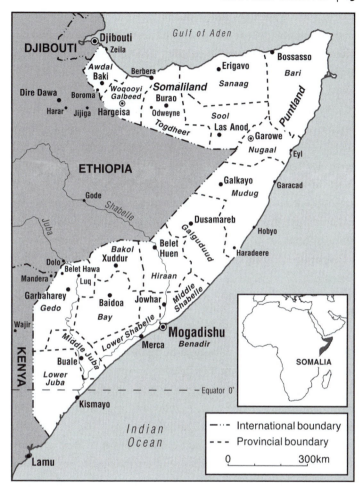

Map 1.1 Somalia

is that Somalis are so easily identifiable as a people or even a 'race';[1] unlike the populations of almost every other country in sub-Saharan Africa, most Somalis have a common ethnicity, religion, language and, to a large extent, culture.

There are of course exceptions. There are minority groups

in Somalia who have traditionally been marginalized by the majority population; some of them have suffered disproportionate violence during periods of conflict. The largest minority is the Bantu or Jareer, descendants of slaves and settled farmers; the word '*jareer*' literally means 'those with coarse hair'. They have mainly lived and worked as farmers or craftspeople in the fertile inter-riverine region of southern Somalia, but many have been displaced. They are sometimes referred to as *adoon*, the Somali term for 'slave'. Other minority groups include the Benadiri mercantile communities of Arab origin living in coastal areas, religious minorities including a small group of Christians, and occupational groups such as blacksmiths, leather workers and ritual specialists. The minorities speak Somali but generally live as separate communities, and are looked down upon by other Somalis.

Resources

Somalis like to joke that, even without the numerous conflicts they have endured, they live in a hostile environment, and this is what makes them so prone to fighting and violence. Much of the country is harsh, arid scrubland, dotted with camels and other hardy animals, watched over by equally hardy nomads in their relentless search for water and pasture. Livestock has for centuries been the mainstay of the Somali economy, with trading networks stretching across the sea to the Arabian Peninsula, and by land into Kenya and other countries in the region. It is amazing to watch livestock being herded on to huge ships docked at the port of Berbera in Somaliland, great waves of sheep streaming up runways on to the vessel, camels swinging high in the air, suspended from chains with belts around their bellies as they are winched, often two at a time, up on to the deck. Most are taken to Saudi Arabia, where fortunes can be made from their sale, especially during the busy haj period. However, the livestock trade is a precarious business; Saudi Arabia periodically imposes bans on the import of Somali animals, sometimes for years. Poor rainfall and drought are also a near-constant threat.

Although significantly more money is made from the sale of cattle, sheep and goats, by far the most precious form of livestock in Somalia is the camel, which plays a central part in the local culture. A typical rural landscape includes camels wandering among thorn trees, aloe plants, cacti and anthills. Sometimes a single hobbled beast stops vehicular traffic as it stumbles awkwardly across the road; herds of baby camels wander through the scrub, separated from their mothers to stop them suckling; groups of adult beasts munch nonchalantly, watched over by a skinny nomad dressed in simple robes, his arms draped around a stick balanced horizontally across his shoulders.

> We Somalis are completely inseparable from our camels. Historically we have depended on them for milk, meat, money and transport. They were our first form of long-haul transport, carrying all of our worldly belongings on their backs for days without needing a drop of water. Camels are the backbones of the rural areas. Somalis have a sort of romantic relationship with camels because they are so deeply attached to them. Even though the number of nomads is declining, our love for camels will never die. We even write poems about them. (Abdullah Farah, farmer, Somaliland)

Camels have traditionally been used in life's most important transactions. They are used for dowry payments; blood money is often paid in camels or their equivalent in cash, as is compensation for injury. Camels represent the very essence of Somali life; people sing them special praise songs, they speak on their behalf and they impersonate them. The Somali camel has even had its own Facebook page.[2]

One reason why the camel has earned such respect is its ability to endure the difficult environmental conditions in the country. As the Somalia expert John Drysdale writes:

> The Somali camel, a one-humped beast, can go longer without water than any other breed of camel. In the very driest weather it need not be watered more than once every three weeks ... The nomad subsists during this dry period entirely on camel's milk. Not even the morning dew passes between his lips; that he collects to wash himself.[3]

The romance and importance of the Somali camel have also been described eloquently by Professor Lewis:

> Milch camels provide milk for the pastoralist on which alone he often depends for his diet; burden camels, which are not normally ridden except by the sick, transport his collapsible hut or tent and all his worldly possessions from place to place. Camel-hide is used to make sandals to protect his feet on the long treks across the country. But these uses do not in themselves account for the way in which pastoralists value their camels or, despite the long-standing and wide use of money as currency, explain why it is primarily in the size and quality of his camels that a man's substance is most tellingly measured. This striking bias in Somali culture is best expressed briefly by saying that in their social as well as economic transactions the pastoralists operate on a camel standard.[4]

Despite its harsh environment, hardy livestock are not Somalia's only resource. North-eastern Somalia was in ancient times known as the 'Land of Punt' or the 'Land of Fine Scents' because on its arid terrain grow straggly trees whose sap is used to produce frankincense and myrrh. These have been traded for centuries and used as incense in religious rituals by Christians and Muslims the world over. This semi-autonomous region has in recent years reclaimed the name of Puntland, although at the time of writing it was better known for its pirates than its perfume.

In recent years, oil and natural gas reserves have been discovered off the Somali coast but conflict, piracy and the uncertain political situation have prevented their exploitation. On a visit to Somaliland in 2011, I met groups of Norwegians and Saudi Arabians who had come to discuss the possibility of becoming involved in the energy industry. However, the lack of international recognition for the territory has in the past served as a significant obstacle to the development of this sector.

Parts of Somalia are fertile, especially in the south between the country's two main rivers, the Juba and the Shabelle. Farmers have traditionally lived here, growing maize, sorghum, millet and other crops, although agriculture has been severely disrupted by the long years of conflict. Farmers are looked down upon by Somali nomads, who consider their settled way of life as inferior to their own constant wanderings. During colonial times, large banana plantations were developed along the rivers, with most of the fruit sold for export. The banana trade continued for some time during the period of intense conflict following the ousting of President Siad Barre – indeed, the sale of 'blood bananas' helped fund some of the warring factions – but as the years of instability dragged on, the international banana business all but collapsed, with some plantations destroyed during battles between different armed groups. Bananas continue to be an important part of the Somali diet, often eaten as an accompaniment to the main savoury dish.

The long coastline is rich in fish and other marine resources, although nomads have traditionally scorned people who eat fish. There is an old Somali saying about a nomad who vomited every time he met somebody who lived near the sea because just the thought of somebody eating fish made him feel violently unwell. Despite their superior attitudes towards farmers and fishermen, tens of thousands of nomads were forced to take up these occupations when they were resettled by the government after a severe drought in the mid-1970s, which decimated their livestock and destroyed their way of life. They found this change of lifestyle humiliating.

The disdain for fish has led to serious problems during periods of hunger or famine because some Somalis refuse to eat it, even when nothing else is available. Foreign aid workers have spoken of their frustration about people's refusal to eat fish or feed it to their children during the conflict in the early 1990s when most other food had run out in Mogadishu, a seaside capital, with an ocean full of fish. I remember arriving at the airport in Mogadishu during the height of the civil war; people were starving but box after box of seafood was being loaded on to planes bound for Saudi Arabia, where it was sold for high prices as a delicacy.

Although an increasing number of Somalis are eating fish, the maritime industry faces another problem. Foreign trawlers have taken advantage of the collapse of central authority to plunder Somali waters; many pirates say it is the robbing of their seas by foreigners which led them to abandon fishing and take up piracy. In his book *Somalia: The New Barbary?* Martin Murphy describes the extent of the problem:

> After 1991 there was no force to protect these fishing grounds. Foreign boats moved in aggressively to catch tuna, shark and ray fins, lobster, shrimp and whitefish ... The fishing vessels came from, or were financed by, companies located in local states such as Yemen, Egypt, Saudi Arabia, and Pakistan and from others around the world known as distant water fishing nations including Taiwan, China, Japan, South Korea and Thailand, and from the European Union, Spain in particular, whose ships often flew the flags of Belize or other 'flag of convenience' states in order to circumvent EU restrictions.[5]

Nomads

Perhaps the greatest resource Somalia has is its people. Because they live in such an unforgiving environment, they are hugely resourceful, resilient and enterprising. Somalis have little to rely on apart from themselves and their strong clan networks. Wherever they go in the world, they survive and often thrive by engaging in business. Despite the many years of conflict and other difficulties that have led so many Somalis to settle abroad, or live for years in refugee or displaced people's camps, many of them have clung with fierce pride to elements of their traditional nomadic culture, even though it is a way of life that many of them have lost for ever.

It is difficult to put numbers on anything in Somalia, but it has been estimated that between 60 and 70 per cent of Somalis are nomads or have a nomadic affiliation.[6] Unlike in many other African countries where nomadic communities are looked down upon or viewed with suspicion, the Somalis, even those living in towns and cities at home and abroad, tend to idealize this way of life, maintaining contact with and interests in the nomadic lifestyle. I have on several occasions sat with Somali friends in London, Nairobi, Hargeisa and Mogadishu, as they speak in a dreamlike way about their camels and their lucky cousins who still live as nomads. The highest admiration of all is reserved for the camel herders, who they say are the finest and fiercest of all Somalis. They have ironic but humorous contempt for what they describe as the indulgent, lazy ways of urban dwellers like themselves. Professor Lewis explains how central nomadism has remained to the Somali way of life:

> It cannot be emphasised too strongly that pastoral nomadism constitutes the economic base of the vast bulk of the Somali population, and the manifestations of the nomadic lifestyle and traditions pervade almost all aspects of Somali life. In contrast

to nomadic minorities in other countries, Somalia's nomads are not cut off from the life of urban centres or culturally and socially separated from the majority of urban residents, civil servants and other government employees such as members of the armed forces. From the president downwards, at all levels of government and administration, those living with a modern lifestyle in urban conditions have brothers and cousins living as nomads in the interior and regularly have shares in joint livestock herds. Civil servants commonly invest in livestock, including camels, that are herded by their nomadic kinsmen.[7]

It is vital to understand the survival of the nomad 'ethos' in Somalia because it helps explain the country's resistance to a centralized system of government. As Lewis explains, 'a hierarchical pattern of authority is foreign to pastoral Somali society which in its customary process of decision-making is democratic almost to the point of anarchy'.[8] The nomadic way of life also explains why national borders and the very idea of a 'country' do not mean much to many Somalis. Nomads have traditionally moved along routes followed for centuries by their sub-clans, regardless of frontier posts, although these have been disrupted by the conflict.

Although urbanization and the long years of war and drought mean that many Somalis have given up their nomadic lifestyle, it is not uncommon for urban families to send their sons to the bush for several months to live with nomadic relatives as a way of 'toughening them up'. The Somali journalist Mohamed Adde, who helped me research this book, describes how he was sent away from Mogadishu at a young age to live with his nomadic cousins:

> We had one meal every twenty-four hours, and that consisted of fresh camel's milk. We ate meat once a fortnight. We drank 'wild water', sucking it from fruit and roots. We slept on the

bare ground, clearing an area of bushes to make sure we slept on clean sand where nobody had trodden before, but always checking for snakes before we lay down. Nomads carry very little. They have a wooden pot for water, which is not used for drinking but for religious ablutions because praying is more important than drinking; they have a wooden headrest called a *barkin* to use as a pillow at night. They carry a gun or stick, and always have a dagger tucked into the belt at the back. Nowadays, they all have mobile phones, which are very useful for finding out the latest market prices for livestock and keeping in touch with the clan. Nomads wear two pieces of white cloth wrapped around their bodies, and have sandals made from camel hide or old tyres.

Nomads are natural soldiers; they live a warrior lifestyle. They are tough, unencumbered by possessions, and used to travelling great distances on foot. They can easily adapt to the life of a fighter, be it an Islamist militant, a member of a clan militia or a government soldier. Some nomads will simply fight for whoever pays the most. There have been consistent reports of the Islamist group al-Shabaab recruiting fighters directly from the government army and vice versa simply by offering them higher wages.

Nomadic women also lead a punishing existence. While the men are away with the cattle and camels, they settle temporarily in camps with children and the elderly, tending she-camels, sheep and goats. As the Somalia expert Michael Walls explains, despite playing a key role in urban and rural economies, most Somali women have a 'secondary' role in society:

> One, though by no means the only, means of consolidating exogenous alliances is through marriage, and consequently there is an informal yet frequently pivotal role for women, who can act as go-betweens between their clan of birth and the one they entered through marriage. While Somali women have long

played a vital role in facilitating communication, mobilising resources, and applying informal pressure in favour of specific outcomes, the formal socio-political process is overwhelmingly the preserve of men.[9]

The Somali author Nuruddin Farah has a particular sensitivity towards the position of women in Somali society. The title of his first published novel, *From a Crooked Rib*, is taken from a Somali proverb about women:

God created Woman from a crooked rib;
and any one who trieth to
straighten it, breaketh it.

The book tells the story of Ebla, a girl from the country, who runs away to town and ends up in various unequal and complicated relationships with men:

She loathed this discrimination between the sexes: the idea
that boys lift up the prestige of the family and keep the
family's name alive. Even a moron-male costs twice as much
as two women in terms of blood-compensation. As many as
twenty or thirty camels are allotted to each son. The women,
however, have to wait until their fates give them a new status
in life: the status of marriage. A she-camel is given to the son,
as people say 'tied to his navel' as soon as he is born. 'Maybe
God prefers men to women,' she told herself.[10]

In a later novel, *Gifts*, Farah writes about the position of the protagonist, whose name is Duniya:

It was when she thought of herself as a woman and thought
about the female gender ... that Duniya felt depressed. The
landmarks of her journey through life from infancy to adult-
hood were marked by various 'stations', all of them owned by
men, run and dominated by men. Did she not move from her

father's home directly into Zubair's [her first husband]? Did she not flee Zubair's right into Shiriye's [her second husband]? … Meanwhile, her elder brother Abshir's omnipresent, benevolent, well-meaning shadow fell on every ramshackle structure she built, pursuing every move she made, informing every step she took: Abshir being another station, another man. Now there was Bosaaso [her boyfriend]. *Morale della storia?* Duniya was homeless, like a great many women the world over. And as a woman she was property-less.[11]

Nothing much has changed for many women in Somalia. The minister for women in the transitional government, Maryam Qasin, said in 2011 that 'the most dangerous thing a woman can do in Somalia today is to become pregnant' owing to the ongoing insecurity and lack of basic maternity services. The danger is not over even for those women who do manage to safely deliver a child; the World Health Organization said in the same year that almost half the victims of weapons-related injuries in Somalia were children under the age of five.

2 Women soldiers in the transitional government army (Mohamed Moalimuu)

Poetry

Perhaps because their material life is so sparse, Somali nomads have a rich oral culture. Professor Lewis says it is in oratory and poetry 'that Somalis' most impressive artistic achievements are to be found. This aesthetic specialisation fits well with the nomadic bias of a people used to travelling light with their livestock and few material encumbrances, but a richly compensating gift of language. Somalis are born talkers, poets and story-tellers.'[12]

Somalis have been quick to adapt their traditional oral culture to modern technology. They have an insatiable appetite for radio and television; it is said that, during the height of the civil war in the 1990s, people would stop fighting to listen to Somali-language broadcasts on the BBC World Service. They are also obsessed with the Internet; there are hundreds of websites devoted to Somali news, politics and culture. Poetry continues to play a central role in Somali life, with the works of dead and living poets used to praise, insult, encourage, remember, and to comment on current events.

One of the most famous poets is the 'Mad Mullah', Seyyid Mohamed Abdulle Hassan, who lived from about 1860 to 1921. Many of his poems were used as a language of war, to motivate his fighters and terrify his enemies. He also wrote about other elements of Somali life, including the harsh natural environment. This is an excerpt from his poem *A Land of Drought*:

All these were mine –
Camels, newly-calved, cattle plump of flesh,
A stock of sheep and goats,
Skimmed milk enough to plunge my mouth in deep and gulp
   it down.
An abundance of wealth …

As I set down my family on this plain of Doodi
I saw that even a goat would go hungry here …

And where if a rotting carcass meets my sight
It proves to be that of a man or a woman or a child.

This is a place without one patch of ground
Where the wild game herds could graze,
It is a place where beasts must pluck
Small mouthfuls here and there of scrub and straw,
It is a place of no abiding use,
A place where teeth will find no food to chew![13]

Love, war, women and camels seem to feature in almost equal measure in Somali poetry. Below is an excerpt from the work of another poet, Omar Hussein Ostreeliya, who died in the 1960s. He was nicknamed 'Ostreeliya' because he spoke constantly about Australia, a land he had visited during his extensive travels around the world. *In Praise of Weris* refers to beauty and bullets, almost in the same breath:

Her sandals, solidly-soled and finely-balanced,
Are cut from the finest cow-flank leather.
As she passes along an encampment lane
The clatter of her jewels
Makes the sound of bullets or a cracking whip.[14]

The use of poetry to comment on current events can be risky, even life-threatening. The young poet Abdirashid Omar wrote a poem, *Fatwo*, or 'The Decree', in December 2009 following the suicide bombing in Mogadishu of a graduation ceremony for medical students which killed more than twenty people, including government ministers. Al-Shabaab said they would kill him if he did not either withdraw the poem or write another one praising them. He refused and had to go into hiding.

Somalia's consuming plague;
The inferno that did ensue;
And the guns that burn and blaze;

For sport, and the sake of fun ...

... the fanatics of Shabaab;
Whatever good they flaunt;
Via blasts and fear of bombs;
Is blight, and ravaging plagues;
With no grounds in the Holy Book ...[15]

Traditional poetry and song remain a central part of the Somali way of life, but they have also been adapted into more contemporary styles, especially rap, to which oral culture is especially well suited. The Somali-Canadian singer K'naan, for example, has gained widespread popularity as a modern rap artist. Young Somalis in Britain fused the traditional with the modern when they released a special song calling for the release of a British couple who were kidnapped by Somali pirates in 2009.

In addition to the highly creative poems, jokes, insults and proverbs there are the witty, imaginative and sometimes disarmingly frank nicknames given to many Somalis. Some prominent people are known only by their nicknames; one powerful clan leader is called *Shaati Gaduud*, which translates as 'Red Shirt', another as *Indha Adde*, which means 'White Eyes', referring to his habit of rolling his eyes back in his head, showing only the whites of his eyes. President Siad Barre was known as *Afweyne*, or 'Big Mouth'. The name *Siad* itself means 'Black Spots' or 'Black Markings'. Other common nicknames include *Guray*, 'The Left Handed', *Genay*, 'The Missing Tooth' or 'The Chipped Tooth', *Roble*, which means 'Born on a Rainy Day', and *Geelle*, 'The Owner of Many Camels', a name often given to people who are tall and strong. Women are sometimes given nicknames; these are usually flattering, such as *Sorkorey*, meaning 'Sugar' or 'Sweet', *Luul*, 'Diamond', and *Cod Weyne*, 'The Rich Voiced'.[16]

Somalis also have a long list of names they use to describe foreigners, often in a derogatory way. White people are referred to as *gaalo*, meaning 'non-believers' or 'infidels'; this term is also used to describe other non-Muslims. A special term is reserved for Americans and Russians; they are called *kaba-weyne* or 'Big Shoes', referring to their large physiques and clumsy ways. Arabs are sometimes called *dhega-cas* or 'Red Ears', and Chinese are called *indha-yar*, which means 'Small Eyes'.

Qat

Another central part of life in Somalia is *qat*. This narcotic leaf, grown in Kenya and Ethiopia, is packed into people's cheeks and chewed for hours, usually in the afternoons and evenings. It is so popular and addictive that, throughout the years of civil war, *qat* planes have been flown into Somalia, landing on rough airstrips in remote and dangerous parts of the country. The *qat* trade is worth tens of millions of dollars a year, and does not seem to have been in the least bit disrupted by the conflict.

The arrival of *qat* creates an atmosphere of hysteria. In Eastleigh, the Somali district of Nairobi, trucks rush in from the central Kenyan region of Meru, where the leaf is grown. There are manic scenes as dealers separate the fresh bunches of *qat* into piles for export to Europe and for local sale. Eastleigh has a special '*qat* street', lined with kiosks with bunches of *qat* leaves hanging from their tin roofs, the finest quality selling for about US$30 a bunch. The road is full of tea shops, people relaxing on chairs or sprawled on the pavement, smoking cigarettes, drinking water, soft drinks or tea, and chewing *qat*. These tea shops, a key part of Somali life all over the world, are like mini-parliaments, with people arguing noisily about local politics and world events. When they open their mouths to speak, they sometimes spray pale green chewed-up leaves and stalks into the air. They look a bit like cows chewing their cud, their cheeks distorted by the large quantity of leaves packed inside them:

I am a champion *qat* chewer. We Somalis believe that *qat* is the best form of stress management. It completely removes worries from the mind. *Qat* is stimulating but it is also relaxing. When I chew it, I see a wonderful life passing in front of my eyes. When I don't chew it, I feel alone. Chewing *qat* helps me speak deeply and steadily. Some people say chewing makes you crazy, but I don't believe it. Even if it does affect my health, I don't care, because it makes me feel so good. We always joke about chewers, saying 'you look like a goat', 'you look like a camel'. Senior chewers like myself find our *qat*-chewing moments the most comfortable of our lives. (Malele, *qat* chewer, Eastleigh, Kenya)[17]

In the bustling markets of Somaliland's capital, Hargeisa, veiled women stand behind stalls, painted with pictures of green leaves. They sell bunches of *qat* in blue plastic bags to their male clients; one 'side effect' of *qat* is litter; much of Somaliland is bathed in a pale blue shimmer, as plastic bags discarded by chewers catch in the thorn trees, fluttering in the hot breeze. A psychiatrist, Aden Ismail, told me how many of his patients suffer from *qat*-induced psychosis; he described how he had just come from a house in Hargeisa where three brothers were kept chained to the walls to stop them attacking other family members or running off to buy more *qat*.

Greater Somalia

The powerful sense of Somali identity and culture extends way beyond the boundaries of Somalia and Somaliland; acknowledging its existence is essential to any understanding of the 'Somali problem' and the politics of the wider region.

Many Somalis believe they have been short-changed in terms of territory. Somalia is different from most parts of Africa, where several different ethnic groups live within individual countries, often competing with each other for power and resources. The

Somali people, by contrast, are present in a far larger part of the Horn of Africa than that defined by their national boundaries. If the Somali state were to include all of the land with majority Somali populations it would be significantly larger than present-day Somalia, including the self-declared republic of Somaliland. Lewis states that 'Somalis form one of the largest single ethnic blocks in Africa ... and live in continuous occupation of a great expanse of territory covering almost 400,000 square miles'.[18]

The Somali national flag features a white star on a sky-blue background; the five points on the star represent the five regions of 'Greater Somalia', a land that has never existed as a recognized nation-state, but one that many Somalis see as their rightful homeland and have, at times, fought to establish.

However, the idea of a grand unification of the Somali people is little more than a fantasy. 'Greater Somalia' has never existed as a single entity, not even before the continent was carved up in the colonial 'Scramble for Africa'. With a principally nomadic population, Somalis were constantly on the move with their live-stock, in small groups bound together largely by ties of blood and marriage. There were no strong material, political or social needs for a defined Somali nation-state, even though the Somalis themselves were so clearly identifiable as a separate people.

'Greater Somalia' includes parts of all of Somalia's neighbours, so the desire for such a territory represents a potential threat to all of them. Three of the points on the Somali star represent north-eastern Kenya, eastern Ethiopia and Djibouti, all of which have substantial ethnic Somali populations. The other two points represent Somalia and the self-declared republic of Somaliland (see Map 1.2).

The fact that the Somali people live in an area far larger than the Somali state means that, throughout the region's history, irredentist claims have led to an almost permanent state of instability in the Horn of Africa. The dream of a 'Greater Somalia'

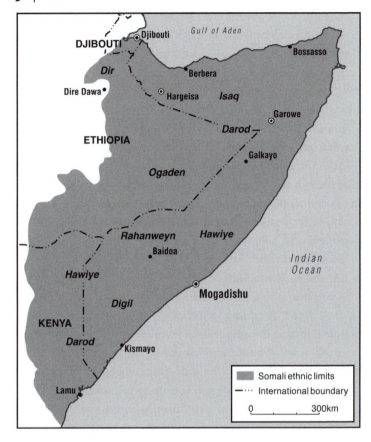

Map 1.2 'Greater Somalia' and geographical distribution of major clans (after Lewis 2002 [1980])

existed for the warrior poet Seyyid Mohamed Abdulle Hassan. Although he never succeeded in establishing such a territory, he sowed the seeds of the idea of fighting for a 'Greater Somalia' into the minds of generations of Somalis to come.

Since independence in 1960, other leaders, including President Siad Barre, have threatened their neighbours with expansionist rhetoric. This has on occasion led to armed conflict that has often ended badly for Somalia and has not resulted in any permanent territorial gains. The most devastating example of this was the war against Ethiopia declared by Siad Barre in 1977, which ended in humiliating defeat, and sowed the seeds of his downfall.

The dream of a 'Greater Somalia' endures to this day; Somali Islamist groups, including al-Shabaab, use it as part of their ideological ammunition and as a rallying cry to attract support. This backfired in 2006 when a leader of the Union of Islamic Courts, Sheikh Hassan Dahir Aweys, threatened to seize the Somali region of Ethiopia. By the end of the year, Ethiopia had invaded Somalia, driving the UIC from power.

Successive conflicts and environmental challenges have led hundreds of thousands of Somalis to leave their country, either as refugees or economic migrants. The United Nations estimated in 2009 that about one million Somalis lived outside the country out of a total population of approximately ten million people.[19] These figures should be treated with caution owing to the difficulty of gathering statistics in and about Somalia, and to the destruction of so many government documents during the conflict.

Somalis have settled in neighbouring Kenya, Ethiopia and Djibouti, and elsewhere in Africa. Others have gone to Yemen, the Gulf states and Saudi Arabia. There are also substantial Somali communities in the United States, Canada, Australia and Europe, especially Great Britain, Holland, Italy and Scandinavian countries. Somalis are a truly globalized people, and they have taken full advantage of modern technology to communicate with and support each other wherever they are in the world. The Internet, mobile phones and the ability to transfer money electronically have, in a sense, led to the creation of a virtual 'Greater Somalia' that extends far beyond the five points of the Somali star. Even though 'Greater Somalia' has never existed as a country, it persists as an inspirational vision for many Somalis today, who see themselves as part of a great 'Somali nation' that stretches beyond frontiers.

Countering the expansionist ideals, there exist equally powerful forces tearing the country apart from within. It is one of the great Somali contradictions that, in diametric opposition to the dream of a 'Greater Somalia', are clan and other divisions that have led to extreme fragmentation within the country itself. These forces had won the upper hand by the early years of the twenty-first century; Somalia is divided into a number of mini-states, some more successful than others. The fact that Somalia has broken apart despite being so homogenous in terms of ethnicity, language, religion and culture means, once again, that common ways of understanding or analysing political difficulties in Africa do not apply. Many of the problems of Nigeria or Sudan, for example, can broadly be explained by differences of religion and ethnicity, although economic and other factors also play a role. Those of Somalia cannot be analysed in this way; they need to be understood on their own terms.

The country that became the independent nation of Somalia in July 1960 was one of the most short-lived on the continent; it lasted as a viable entity for little more than thirty years. The north-western region of Somaliland became a self-declared republic in 1991, although it has not been internationally recognized; Puntland in the north-east has its own government and is relatively autonomous; many other parts of the country operate on their own terms, frequently changing hands between different interest groups, and with unstable, shifting boundaries (see Map 1.3). Some are controlled by Islamist groups, some are affiliated with clans, others have self-declared 'presidents' who live in the diaspora and have rarely or never been there. In 2011, parts of the capital, Mogadishu, and a few other areas were controlled by a weak transitional government backed by peacekeepers from the African Union. This constantly shifting situation makes life very difficult for Somalis, who frequently have to adjust their lifestyles and behaviour according to who holds power in their region,

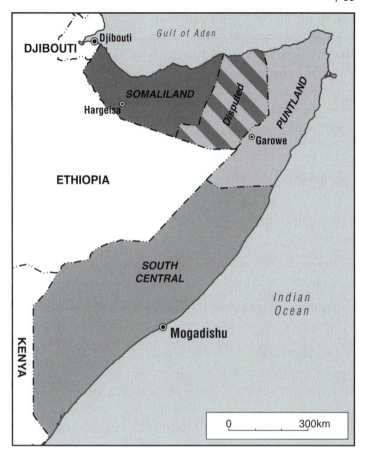

Map 1.3 Main sub-divisions of Somali territory

aware that, at any moment, another group may move in and take control.

The clan

The most obvious force dividing Somalis is the clan, which knits groups of people together into distinct units, often in opposition to other similar clan or lineage groups. The existence of clan

ties has always served as a formidable obstacle to the formation
of a stable, modern nation-state in Somalia; it explains in part the
failure of internal and external efforts to 'unite' Somalia under
the authority of a central government in Mogadishu.

During my research for this book, I asked several Somalis
about the role of the clan. This sample of responses shows what
a contentious issue it is:

You are very rude to ask about clans; they don't exist. (Omar
Mohamed, businessman, Mogadishu)

The clan is the centre of the Somali universe. It determines
everything about us. (Aisha Mariam, community worker,
Hargeisa)

To view Somalia in terms of the clan is to follow a prehistoric
approach. (Yonis Hassan, businessman, Baidoa)

The only way to understand Somalia is to understand the clan.
(Yusuf Nur, elder, Mogadishu)

One of the most important things to understand about Somali
clans is that they are fluid and ambiguous. Somalis cannot easily
be divided into clearly defined clan categories because the clans
themselves are so fragmented; they split into sub-clans, which can
then divide further and further (see Figure 1.1). Alliances between
these almost infinitely divisible groups shift frequently, making
it very difficult for outsiders to understand what is going on. A
seemingly united clan can split into two or more sub-clans, which
turn on each other; former friends or 'brothers' become enemies
overnight, and 'enemies' can equally quickly become friends.

This happened in 2006 when a group of warlords and businessmen formed the Alliance for the Restoration of Peace and
Counter-Terrorism (ARPCT) to resist the growing influence of
the coalition of sharia courts in Mogadishu. The ARPCT is
reported to have received significant support and funding from

SOMALI CLAN FAMILIES

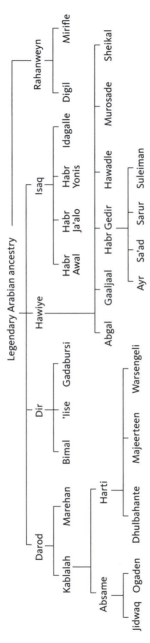

This is a simplified diagram of Somali clan families (following Lewis 1961 and Bradbury 2008). It includes sub-clans mentioned in the book and omits others. It does not offer a definitive picture. A book by a Somali author, Muxamed Ibrahim Muxamed, 'Liiq-Liiqato' (*Taariikhda Soomaaliya*, 2000, Mogadishu) lists some 500 clans and sub-clans over seventeen pages.

Figure 1.1 Somali clan families

the CIA in the United States, which had been led to believe that the sharia courts represented an Islamist terrorist threat. The Americans and others were frequently baffled by the sudden defection of ARPCT leaders to the courts' movement, and their equally unexpected return to the ARPCT. The constant shifting of alliances is endemic to the conflict, and must always be taken into account by anyone trying to understand Somalia.

The BBC Somali service first introduced me to the existence of clans in the early 1990s, during the worst of the fighting in southern and central Somalia after the fall of Siad Barre. I felt I was in an advanced mathematics lesson as they drew me diagrams resembling endlessly branching trees, with a confusion of arrows showing the complex alliances that formed temporarily between the clans. Almost as soon as I felt I was beginning to understand the situation, everything would change. A sub-clan would divide into two sub-sub-clans, with names I had never heard of before. A previously united group would split, its members killing each other with abandon. I also realized that different people in the Somali service would draw me conflicting diagrams of the same situation, depending on their own clan allegiances. There would sometimes be fierce debates and arguments between the staff; some involving humorous attacks on particular clans, others that did not involve humour at all.

It is not only Somalis who argue about the clan; non-Somali academics and other experts are equally divided. Some scholars put the clan at the centre of their analysis; others argue that different factors, such as socio-economic relationships, have played a more important role in shaping Somalia. As the subject of the clan has been given so much attention in other literature, I do not intend to go into great detail about it beyond the next few pages. It will inevitably resurface in other chapters as I believe it often plays a central role in Somali life; as the anthropologist Virginia Luling explains, clans are 'not only good to fight with (or play politics or do business with), but good to think with'.[20] It is impossible to understand Somalia without being aware of clans; it also helps to know which clan individuals belong to, although not all Somalis are willing to disclose this information.

Even attempting to name the main clans in Somalia can end in argument; the 2002–04 Somali peace conference proposed a clan quota that has been used by recent administrations as a guide for how to distribute power. Known as the '4.5 formula', it states that the four main clans are the Darod, Dir, Hawiye and Rahanweyn. The '0.5' refers to all the minority clans. This formula has not been accepted by all groups, and is seen as offensive by some who believe their clans have not been adequately represented.

The importance of the clan has, in some ways, been blurred by recent developments, especially the rise of Islamist groups such as al-Shabaab. But it has traditionally been the basis of the organizational and legal structure of Somali society, especially among the nomads. As people were almost constantly on the move, kinship groups traced through the male line formed the bedrock of society. Bloodlines told people who they were and where they stood in relation to others. Many Somalis can still recite long lists of their male ancestors; this is a central part of their oral culture, and allows them to place themselves in precise positions within society. When nomads meet each other in the bush, they often identify themselves by recounting their lineage, which is in some ways similar to a passport; the ability to name ancestors can, on occasion, be a matter of life or death. As John Drysdale explains, Somalis have a profound knowledge of their lineage history: 'Every one of them, from the age of eight years, can recite his or her genealogy through the male line, some twenty or thirty generations back, to a common ancestor.'[21]

In his many books on Somalia, Professor Lewis gives much attention to the clan, and, as he sees it, its key role in Somali life:

It is their lineage genealogies which direct the lines of political alliance and division. Although Somalis sometimes compare the functions of their genealogies to a person's address in Europe, to understand their true significance it has to be realised that far more is at stake here than mere pride of pedigree. These genealogies define the basic political and legal status of the individual in Somali society at large and assign him a specific place in the social system.[22]

As Lewis mentions, the clan has also traditionally served as the basis for the judicial system in Somalia. The strongest ties within a clan are those between a group of relatives, usually numbering from a few hundred to a few thousand, who are united by a contractual alliance that obliges them to pay and receive 'blood' money or *diya*. This system originated among Somali nomads who often fought each other over scarce grazing and water resources. The mechanism for resolving these conflicts is known as *xeer*, and involves groups of Somali elders holding long discussions or *shir* to work out how much compensation should be paid by each group. The numerous Somali peace conferences, and the House of Elders in the self-declared republic of Somaliland, are in some ways extensions of the traditional *shir*. The existence of a traditional legal system, coupled with the sharia courts, has proved very useful for Somalis during the past twenty years of conflict, providing a ready-made substitute for the state legal system, which has virtually collapsed in many parts of the country.

There have over time been several attempts to break the spirit of the clan. The rise of Islamist groups in some ways eclipsed the importance of the clan because militias were, on the surface, united according to different religious affiliations, rather than blood ties. There is the al-Qaeda-linked al-Shabaab, the slightly more moderate Hizbul Islam, which was taken over by al-Shabaab in 2011, and the Sufi group Ahlu Sunna Wa Jamaa. However, these groups, particularly their leadership, have to some degree become associated with individual clans or sub-clans.

The most deliberate and concerted effort to eliminate the clan came during Siad Barre's experiment with 'scientific socialism' in the 1970s, when Somalia was allied with the Soviet Union. His ferociously nationalistic, anti-Western ideology would not tolerate clannishness, which was portrayed, at least publicly, as an anachronistic impediment to the building of a modern nation. The clan was officially banned, and there were public burnings and burials of effigies representing the clan. Clan chiefs and elders were renamed 'peace-seekers' in an effort to dilute their authority and to rid them of any association with their lineages. Siad Barre tried to replace the complex clan hierarchies with a personality cult. He promoted himself as 'the father of the nation'; the country was plastered with images of 'Comrade Siad', many of them displayed as a trinity alongside portraits of Marx and Lenin.

Despite his anti-clan rhetoric, Siad Barre was privately seeking to promote the interests of his own Marehan clan and its allies; this was known as the 'MOD', an alliance of Darod sub-clans, the Marehan, the Ogaden and the Dhulbahante. This provoked great hostility among other clans, and eventually led to civil war. In the north-west the Isaq clan and others formed the rebel Somali National Movement; in the north-east, the Majerteen and other Darod clans formed the Somali Salvation Democratic Front; and in the south, the Hawiye formed the United Somali Congress. After some years, these groups succeeded in driving Siad Barre from power.

The Union of Islamic Courts also lost support when it started to become too closely associated with the interests of one clan, or, in this case, sub-clan. Even though the origins of the UIC lay in a loose affiliation of sharia courts, representing a number of different clans and sub-clans, it was increasingly perceived as a vehicle to further the ambitions of the Ayr sub-clan of the Hawiye. It is debatable whether the fiery chairman of the shura council of the UIC, Sheikh Hassan Dahir Aweys, and the leader of the al-Shabaab courts militia, Adan Hashi Ayro, harboured supremacist clan ambitions, but the fact that they were perceived as doing so was enough to lose them the support of many non-Ayr members.

However hard people try to eliminate clannishness from Somali politics, they ultimately fail. The clan is unlikely to disappear; it is preserved in the tradition of recounting one's ancestry, in poetry and elsewhere. People can reactivate their clan identities whenever the need arises; it provides a form of insurance, a ready-made social structure, and trusted ties for business and other transactions. A single person can choose from a variety of clan or sub-clan identities, each with a different set of alliance options. In some ways, Somalis are trapped by their clan, as it can identify them with particular factions or religious movements to which they have no desire to belong. For instance, the association of the Ayr sub-clan with violent Islamist groups means Ayr members are often labelled as extremists because of their clan identity, not their personal beliefs.

Retreating into the clan can serve both as a form of protection and a source of danger. Clans can become fighting groups or mini-armies, as they did in the late 1980s and the 1990s. Even though the Hawiye clan initially united in opposition to Siad Barre, it rapidly divided into opposing sub-clans after his downfall, leading to some of the bloodiest fighting Mogadishu has ever seen. These opposing sub-clans fought street by street, alley by alley, for control of the capital. Mogadishu became a divided city, a 'green line' splitting the south, controlled by the Habr-Gedir sub-clan led by the warlord Mohamed Farah Aideed, from the north, which was controlled by the Abgal sub-clan under Ali Mahdi Mohamed. The same thing happened, to a less destructive extent, in Somaliland. The Isaq united to form the Somali National Movement to fight Siad Barre, but after the territory declared itself independent, a number of mini-wars broke out between Isaq sub-clans.

The aim of this chapter has been to show that there is more to Somalia than war, hunger, Islamist extremism and piracy. Most media reports and much of foreign policy do not see beyond these elements; unless they do, they will neither portray the reality of Somalia, nor will they be of much help in trying to address the many problems in the country. The fact that Somalia was starting to fall apart as a functioning state well before the ousting of Siad Barre suggests that a highly centralized Mogadishu-focused system of government is not the solution. The United States and others are slowly beginning to wake up to this, adopting in 2010 a 'two-track' approach to Somalia, whereby increased support is given to more 'successful' regions like Somaliland and Puntland while support continues for the transitional government in Mogadishu.

2 | HISTORY

The recent years of state collapse in Somalia cannot be properly understood without looking farther back into the country's history. Many aspects surrounding the fall of Siad Barre and the subsequent failure to establish effective central authority can be explained in part by trends and events in Somalia's past, as well as a deeper understanding of Somali culture and society as outlined in Chapter 1.

What is difficult to understand is the apparent inability or reluctance of many foreign governments, international institutions and Somali politicians to recognize that they keep repeating the same mistakes. They seem to be stuck on a treadmill, unable or unwilling to step off and try something new, despite the fact that there are readily available examples of 'getting Somalia right', such as some aspects of life under the Union of Islamic Courts and the experience of Somaliland.

In this brief overview of Somali history, certain patterns and themes start to emerge that are almost as relevant to the situation in 2011 as they were in the past. In my research for this book, I studied books about Somalia written several decades ago; as I read them, I could not help wishing that more people would learn from the country's history. It seems as if little has changed since the 1960s when John Drysdale wrote: 'Ironically, Somali history has demonstrated that serious disorders have been traced, not to any malfunction of the Somali system of authority, but to the unimaginative application of alien systems of government which have inadvertently undermined it.'[1]

Pre-colonial

There are three main themes to the early history of Somalia: contact, conflict and expansion. Its long coastline and position on the north-eastern edge of sub-Saharan Africa meant Somalia was never part of the 'dark continent'. It has for centuries been in touch with other parts of the world and home to settler communities, especially along its coast. Early historians and Arab geographers refer to the Somalis as a warlike people, who hundreds of years ago began their slow expansion from the coast, westwards towards Ethiopia and south into what is now northern Kenya, displacing other people as they went.

As Professor Lewis explains, the country's long history of contact with the Arab world has led some Somalis to trace their origins to the Quraysh tribe of the founder of Islam, the Prophet Muhammad:

> Traditionally ... Somalis set most store by their Arabian connections and delight in vaunting those traditions which proclaim their descent from noble Arabian lineages and from the family of the prophet. These claims, dismissed by Somali nationalists today as fanciful, are nevertheless part and parcel of the traditional and profound Somali attachment to Islam.[2]

As Lewis suggests, many Somalis do not genuinely believe they are directly related to the Prophet Muhammad, even though they like the idea of a blood connection. Some scholars, such as Harold Nelson, have gone farther than Lewis by questioning whether Somalis have any Arab roots at all: 'Somalis' Arab ancestry may not stand up to careful scrutiny and is probably a result of the efforts of the deeply Islamic Somalis to attach themselves to people of the prophet.'[3]

Regardless of whether or not their Arab roots are genuine, the perception of a deep connection with the Arab world helps explain why many Somalis see themselves as 'other' than sub-Saharan

Africans, and why so many of them have in recent decades looked to the Arab world for opportunity and refuge.

There has been substantial Arab influence on Somalia for hundreds of years. The existence from at least the seventh century of settled Arab merchant communities in coastal towns such as Mogadishu, Zeila and Berbera led to the mixing of Arab and Somali blood through intermarriage, and hastened the penetration of Islam, which was adapted into a distinctly 'Somali-style' Islamic belief system. The walled town of Zeila, on the north-western coast, was a famous centre for Islamic learning and trade. Coffee was brought to the town from the Abyssinian highlands and slaves from the interior of the continent; these were traded for weapons, cloth, iron, pottery, dates and other goods brought to Zeila by boat.

There were other influences too, some even earlier than the Arabs. The Ancient Egyptians, Greeks and Romans travelled to the 'Land of Punt' in north-eastern Somalia to buy frankincense and myrrh. Persian merchants settled on the coast during the ninth and tenth centuries. The Portuguese attacked coastal towns; there was contact with the Ottomans, the Omanis, the Indians and others.

Colonial

During the nineteenth century, the Somalis were dragged into Europe's 'Scramble for Africa' even though they did not have many desirable natural resources for plunder by the colonial powers. They found themselves in the sights of the British, the Italians, the French and neighbouring Ethiopia, which was considered a regional superpower. This was partly due to their strategic geographical location but also because the Somalis themselves were continuing to migrate, colonizing for themselves an ever-greater stretch of territory. They started to encounter resistance from other powers as they pushed farther south and west; as Tom Farer explains, the British colonialists in northern Kenya 'terminated the 900-year march of the Somali nation down the coast of East Africa. Confronted by British power, the Somalis were forced to accept the Tana river as their southern frontier. There it has remained.'[4]

The British also became involved with the north-western part of Somali territory, albeit in a different way. They had little desire to fully colonize the region, but needed its livestock to feed the British base in Aden just a short distance across the sea; Somali livestock continues to this day to be exported across this stretch of water. Between 1884 and 1889, Britain signed a series of treaties with clans in the area, leading to the establishment of the British Protectorate of Somaliland.

Britain got more than it bargained for; its presence on Somali soil so enraged the warrior poet Seyyid Mohamed Abdulle Hassan that, in June 1903, he wrote a threatening letter to the British people:

> If the country [Somaliland] was cultivated, or contained houses or property, it would be worth your while to fight. The country is all jungle and that is no use to you. If you want wood and stone you can get them in plenty. There are also many ant heaps. The sun is very hot. All you can get from me is war, nothing else.[5]

The 'Mad Mullah' was true to his word; he declared a jihad and for twenty years fought Britain and other colonial powers before he was defeated in 1920. Throughout his campaign, the Seyyid tormented his enemies with words as well as weapons, describing himself as a 'wild and stubborn he-camel that knows no harness or bridle'.[6]

In a letter written in 1917 to the British Commissioner in Berbera the Seyyid rejected suggestions that his dervish forces had received assistance from Turkey, and revelled in recent military successes against Britain by the Turko-German alliance:

You know, and I know, what the Turks have done to you and what the Germans have done to you, you of the British Government. The suggestion is that I was weak and I had to look outside for friends; and if, indeed, this were true and I had to look for assistance, it is only because of the British, and the trouble you have given me. It is you who have joined with all the people of the world, with harlots, with wastrels, and with slaves, because you are so weak. But if you were strong you would have stood by yourself as we do, independent and free. It is a sign of your weakness, this alliance of yours with Somalis, menials and Arabs, and Sudanese, and Kaffirs, and Perverts, and Yemenis, and Nubians, and Indians, and Baluchis, and French, and Russians, and Americans, and Italians and Serbians, and Portuguese, and Japanese, and Greeks and cannibals and Sikhs and Banyans, and Moors, and Afghans, and Egyptians. They are strong, and it is because of your weakness, that you have to solicit as does a prostitute.[7]

When his forces killed the British commander, Richard Corfield, in 1913, the Seyyid composed a brutal celebratory poem:

How the valiant Dervishes have slain you;
How they have abandoned your rotting corpse,
with its gaping dagger-wounds to the carrion-eaters.
Tell them how the hyena
has dragged your carcass to its grisly den;
Tell how it tore the muscle and fat from your skeleton;
Tell how crows plucked your sinews
and tendons from the bare bone ...[8]

So fierce was the Seyyid's resistance that in 1919 the British resorted to aerial attacks against him, the first time they had used the air force in sub-Saharan Africa. Almost one hundred years later, foreign powers are still bombing Somali jihadis from the air:

the United States has in the past few years carried out several air strikes against alleged al-Qaeda-linked targets in Somalia.

Farer writes of how Seyyid Mohamed Abdulle Hassan was instrumental in creating the idea of a 'Greater Somalia' whereby all Somalis would be united in one territory: 'He awakened and nourished the idea that beyond the ties of lineage and blood-contract there were bonds among all Somalis which in the modern world must take precedence ... so although he was defeated, he did not entirely fail.'[9]

Shortly after the collapse of the Seyyid's resistance against the colonial ambitions of Britain, France, Italy and Ethiopia, he died from illness. The vast stretch of Africa that he had fought for, and which was seen by many Somalis as their rightful home, had by that time been split up into five distinct colonial units:

- *The Northern Frontier District* This area formed the north-eastern corner of the British colony of Kenya. When Kenya became independent in 1963, the government in Nairobi refused to accept the demands of the predominantly Somali population in the region to break away and become part of the newly independent Republic of Somalia.
- *The Ogaden* This became part of the Ethiopian empire after being conquered by Ethiopia between 1887 and 1895, although it continued to be a disputed area. Previously called the 'Ogaden', it and other predominantly Somali regions of Ethiopia were later referred to as 'Region Five' and the 'Somali Region'.
- *'Côte Française des Somalis' or the 'French Somali Coast'* The French colony became the independent Republic of Djibouti in 1977.
- *British Somaliland* The British protectorate became independent on 26 June 1960, uniting a mere five days later with *Somalia Italiana* to create the Republic of Somalia. It broke away on 18 May 1991 as the self-declared Republic of Somaliland, retaining

the same borders as the British protectorate. The eastern part of the territory is under dispute with the neighbouring region of Puntland.

• *Somalia Italiana* Colonized by Italy, and from 1950 a United Nations trusteeship under Italian administration, the region became independent on 1 July 1960, joining with British Somaliland to form the Republic of Somalia.

The separation of Somalis into different colonial territories made no sense to this predominantly nomadic people, who had never seen much point in boundaries or central government. The Somali poet Faarah Nur was baffled by the fierce foreign competition for Somali territory:

> The British, the Ethiopians and the Italians are squabbling,
> The country is snatched and divided by whoever is stronger,
> The country is sold piece by piece without our knowledge,
> And for me, all this is the Teeth of the Last Days![10]

Around the time of the Second World War, Somalis came closer than ever to achieving their dream of a 'Greater Somalia'. During the 1930s, the Italian Fascist leader, Benito Mussolini, fought to establish an *Africa Orientale Italiana* or 'Italian East African Empire'. Between 1936 and 1941, three points on the Somali star – eastern Ethiopia, the Somaliland Protectorate and *Somalia Italiana* – were under Italian control. The British launched a counter-offensive, and by 1941 controlled four points of the star: the Ogaden, *Somalia Italiana*, Somaliland and north-eastern Kenya. The British foreign minister, Ernest Bevin, proposed that all Somalis should be administered as a single unit and prepared for independence. In June 1946, he suggested to the British House of Commons that the Somali-speaking areas ...

> ... should be lumped together as a trust territory so that
> the nomads should lead their frugal existence with the least

possible hindrance and there might be a real chance of a
decent economic life as understood in that territory ... All I
want to do is to give those poor nomads a chance to live ... It
is to nobody's interest to stop the poor people and cattle there
getting a decent living.

The 'Bevin Plan' never materialized because it was resisted by
the other main post-war powers, France, Russia and the United
States. The four regions under British military control resumed
their former status, apart from the Italian colony, which in 1950
became a United Nations trusteeship to be administered by Italy
for ten years, after which it would become independent.

Perhaps most painful for Somalis was the transfer to Ethiopia
of territories they saw as rightfully theirs. Many Somalis still blame
Britain for transferring control of the Ogaden to Ethiopia in 1948,
and the rich grazing lands known as the Haud and Reserved Area
in the mid-1950s. The presence of a large Somali population in
Ethiopia has proved a constant headache to the authorities there;
the eastern 'Somali region' has for decades been in a state of almost
permanent rebellion, often supported by whoever holds power in
Somalia. In some ways, the special status accorded to Ethiopia
during the colonial period continues today. It has been a 'special
friend' of the United States in its 'War on Terror', particularly on
the Somali front. Ethiopia helped carry out America's 'dirty work'
in Somalia in 2006 by driving out the Union of Islamic Courts,
which was perceived by the USA as a radical Islamist threat.
Ethiopia also had its own strategic reasons for wanting to destroy
the UIC; the courts were considered an ally of Eritrea, which had
recently been involved in a civil war with Ethiopia.

Independence

During the 1940s and 1950s, party political activity was starting
to develop in *Somalia Italiana*; the Somali Youth Club was formed

in 1943, later developing into one of the main political parties, the Somali Youth League. Somalis at the time were, to some degree, being prepared for independence. Municipal elections were held in 1954 and, by 1956, the Italians had handed over much of the administration to the Somalis. In 1960, both Somaliland and *Somalia Italiana* became independent, uniting on 1 July to become the Republic of Somalia. Many were determined that this was only the beginning, that other Somali-dominated territories would join them, uniting the Somali 'nation' into a single state. One of them was the Somali prime minister, Abdirashid Ali Sharmarke, who would later become president:

> Our misfortune is that our neighbouring countries, with whom, like the rest of Africa, we seek to promote constructive and harmonious relations, are not our neighbours. Our neighbours are our Somali kinsmen whose citizenship has been falsified by indiscriminate boundary 'arrangements'. They have to move across artificial frontiers to their pastoral lands. They occupy the same terrain and pursue the same pastoral economy as ourselves. We speak the same language. We share the same creed, the same culture and the same traditions. How can we regard our brothers as foreigners?[11]

The newly independent Somalia first set its sights on the Northern Frontier District in colonial Kenya. The government argued that, 'by racial stock and language, the people of the Northern Frontier District are kindred with the people of The Somali Republic, but alien to the peoples of Kenya', suggesting to the British colonial authorities that the area 'be joined in an act of union with The Somali Republic when Kenya becomes independent'.[12] A British commission found in 1962 that Somalis, who it said made up more than 60 per cent of the population of the region, almost unanimously favoured secession from Kenya and eventual union with Somalia. But most people in Kenya and other newly or soon-to-be independent African countries opposed the idea, afraid it would encourage other secessionist movements on the continent. The idea was shelved, provoking anger from Somalia, which in 1963 temporarily severed diplomatic relations with Britain.

Kenya, like Ethiopia, has over the years faced significant trouble from its Somali population. The words of John Drysdale hold as much relevance today as when he wrote them in 1964: 'Kenya and Ethiopia are faced with an unsubdued, uncooperative, volatile, nomadic people who can move unseen, with pluck and agility, in and out of The Somali Republic, with or without firearms, in full command of their desert environment.'[13]

The British senior colonial official, Lord Renell Rodd, who spent years in the Horn of Africa, believed his government's policy towards Somalia would lead to serious problems in the future:

> If we had been interested enough ... (and if the world had been sensible enough) all the Somalis ... might have remained under our administration. But the world was not sensible enough, and we were not interested enough, and so the only part of Africa which is radically homogeneous has been split into such parts as made Caesar's Gaul the problem and cockpit of Europe for the last two thousand years. And Somaliland will probably become a cockpit of East Africa.[14]

In spite of the disappointment of failing to establish a 'Greater Somalia', the first few years after independence saw the establishment of lively parliamentary democracy in the new republic. The vigorous debates in parliament and hotly contested elections, often with overwhelming numbers of candidates and political parties, seemed to fit well with Somalis' passion for argument and their vibrant oral culture. In 1969, 1,002 candidates from 62 parties contested just 123 seats in the National Assembly. The first nine years of independence were relatively positive and exciting despite the problems that arose as a result of clan frictions, differences between the two former colonies, lack of education and other factors. The political scientist Ali Mazrui writes that during this period Somalia came 'close to being the most open society in post-colonial Africa'.[15]

Dictatorship

Everything changed in 1969. On 15 October, the president, Abdirashid Ali Sharmarke, was killed by a policeman in what appeared to be an act of revenge linked to a clan dispute. Less than a week later, in the early hours of 21 October, the military took over key installations in Mogadishu, banning political parties and arresting senior politicians. The country would henceforth be governed by a Supreme Revolutionary Council led by the head of the army, General Siad Barre. The ringleader of this bloodless coup was to stay in power for more than twenty years.

A form of 'scientific socialism' was introduced, and with it came the attempted eradication of the clan, one of the most fundamental elements of Somali society. It was, said Siad Barre, anathema to the socialist revolution: 'Tribalism and nationalism cannot go hand in hand. It is unfortunate that our nation is rather too clannish: if all Somalis are to go to Hell, tribalism will be their vehicle to get there.'

One of the key slogans for the new Somalia was 'Tribalism divides, Socialism unites'. Somalis were forbidden to refer to each other in terms of their clan, instructed instead to address one another as *jaale*, which meant 'comrade' or 'friend'. Effigies of the clan were symbolically burned or buried. In the spirit of their new communist allies in the Soviet Union and North Korea, Somalis were encouraged to take part in gymnastic displays and public works. In a further effort to sweep away 'old-fashioned', clannish oral culture, a written form of the Somali language was introduced for the first time in 1972. This was followed in 1974 by a mass literacy campaign. As Lewis describes, most secondary schools in the country were closed as more than thirty thousand students and teachers were trucked out to rural areas to teach literacy, basic hygiene and the fundamentals of socialism to the nomads.

> Equipped with blankets, a folding blackboard (which did not open properly), water bottle, and other basic kit and drawing a daily allowance of two Somali shillings, these privileged urban students were to share the fruits of the revolution with their neglected nomadic comrades, staying as guests with nomadic families and repaying hospitality by teaching their hosts to read and write.[16]

It was during this period that conditions in Somalia started to deteriorate significantly. From 1974 to 1975, the country experienced what was at the time the worst drought in its history. In 1977, in a renewed effort to establish a 'Greater Somalia' and possibly to distract people from domestic hardship, Siad Barre declared war on Ethiopia, with the aim of capturing the Ogaden. It was during this conflict that the Soviet Union dramatically changed sides, abandoning Somalia as an ally after an appeal for help from Ethiopia's new Marxist revolutionary leader, Mengistu Haile Mariam, who had in 1974 overthrown the Emperor Haile Selassie. The Soviets supplied their new Ethiopian friends with a vast amount of military assistance, leading to the defeat of Somalia in 1978. The devastation caused by drought and war led growing numbers of Somalis to turn against their president. In a sign of the growing disenchantment, a group of army officers led an abortive coup against Siad Barre in 1978.

The country was beginning to crumble. Siad Barre's efforts to eliminate clannishness backfired; by the 1980s, a number of regional, clan-based rebel movements had been formed. Among the first of these groups was the Somali National Movement (SNM). It was originally a multi-clan force, which later came to represent the interests of the Isaq clan from the former British

Protectorate of Somaliland, who resisted what they felt was marginalization and persecution by the Barre government. The authorities' response to the rebellion was extraordinarily vicious; Siad Barre's ground and air forces carried out such heavy bombardment of the regional capital, Hargeisa, that it was known as the 'Dresden of Africa'. Barely a wall was left standing and almost every roof of every building was blown off or looted. The city was smashed and stripped; its population eventually left, walking all the way to Ethiopia in a biblical-style exodus, as described by Mark Bradbury in his book *Becoming Somaliland*: 'The flight of some 500,000 civilians from northern Somalia to Ethiopia in 1988 was one of the fastest and largest forced movements of people recorded in Africa.'[17]

The May 1988 SNM attacks on Hargeisa and Burao launched the civil war in Somalia, which has continued for more than two decades. Other groups formed elsewhere in the country; the Somali Salvation Democratic Front (SSDF) was established some years earlier in the north-east; the United Somali Congress (USC), which largely represented the interests of the Hawiye clan, was created in south-central Somalia; the Somali Patriotic Movement (SPM) was formed by members of the Ogaden clan. In August 1990, the SNM, SPM and USC met in Ethiopia, and agreed to form a united front against Siad Barre.

By this time, in a situation strikingly similar to that of twenty years later, the central government's control did not extend much further than the capital city. So limited was his power that Siad Barre's opponents referred to him as the 'Mayor of Mogadishu'. Opposition forces closed in and, on 26 January 1991, Barre lost control of the capital, driven out by USC fighters.

State collapse

The fall of Siad Barre did not mark the end of the war. Although an often cruel and harsh dictator was driven from power, since 1990 the majority of Somalis have lived without any effective central leadership; they have lived without a state.

Almost as soon as Siad Barre was ousted, the USC turned on itself. Hawiye unity disintegrated as two of its sub-clans, the Abgal and Habr Gedir, became bitter enemies, and started fighting each other. The British aid worker Murray Watson witnessed the early days of the conflict in 1991:

> There is a lot of fighting and shooting around the presidential palace. I've just been round the hospital which is receiving between fifty and sixty wounded people a day. Doctors are carrying out ten or fifteen amputations every day. I've got blood on my feet. You cannot imagine the carnage. I took some photographs of bodies in the streets just now. There aren't so many bodies because the dogs have eaten most of them. But there are still hands sticking up through the sand. Along the roadside there are impromptu burial grounds where people have been buried where they died. Most of the casualties are civilians; they are women, they are old men, they are children.

This was Somalia and its clan system at its most self-destructive. Instead of leading to peace and the establishment of a fair, democratic system of government, the fall of Siad Barre resulted in senseless conflict, with civilians bearing the worst of the consequences. Dictatorship was replaced by the rule of the warlord, as powerful clan leaders, supported by wealthy businessmen and mini-armies of militiamen, turned much of Somalia into a patchwork of fiefdoms. These groups either fought each other or formed alliances with one another, only to break apart within a short period of time. The unpredictable and fast-moving situation was bewildering for everybody, both inside and outside Somalia.

Visiting Somalia in the early 1990s, it was rare to see a man or teenage boy without a gun. A weapon seemed as essential as a shirt, more vital than a pair of shoes. Wild-eyed, sweating young fighters raced past on Somali-style war wagons known as 'technicals'; these were pick-up trucks or Land Cruisers with their backs sawn off, mounted with a big gun and packed with heavily armed militiamen. The constant shooting and shelling killed tens of thousands of people, injured and displaced many more, and destroyed Mogadishu, once one of the most beautiful cities in Africa. One man who tried to stop the destruction was Omar Salad, who held several senior positions under Siad Barre but had by that time joined the opposition:

> What I saw was terrible, terrible. There was killing, there was looting, there was chaos. People were stealing from houses, they were raping women. It was horrible. I was doing my best to help, to save friends and relatives. The clan militias were fighting with all sorts of weapons: machine guns, rifles, anti-aircraft guns mounted on land cruisers, and katyusha rockets. In no time at all, the heart of the city was destroyed and turned into rubble.
>
> I went to the National Theatre, a very beautiful building, which was being cannibalised, completely stripped bare. I took some of my bodyguards to the theatre and ordered them to fire above the heads of the looters. This scared the thieves away. I then ordered two of my bodyguards to stay there permanently in order to save the theatre.
>
> I went to a restaurant in Mogadishu where I saw people using secret government documents as napkins. They were even using them in the toilets. I gave the restaurant owner some money and took the precious documents away. I discovered the same thing was happening in restaurants all over the city, so I rescued as many papers as I could. I ended up with 175 files of government documents.

Accompanying the death and destruction came hunger. It soon

developed into what was essentially a man-made famine; much of Somalia's most fertile land between the Juba and Shabelle rivers had become a battleground for rival factions. Members of settled farming communities were either killed, forced to flee or to join militias. Food could not be moved around the country without being looted by clan militias. People started to starve to death, especially in parts of southern and central Somalia. Omar Salad broke down when he told me about the first time he visited the worst-affected area, known as the 'Triangle of Death':

> I saw hundreds of children lying in long rows along the tarmac
> road. They were naked, they were skeletons, but they weren't
> dead. They were still alive, but about to die. When I asked
> what all these hundreds of children were doing like this on
> the road, I was told their parents had died of famine. I wept.
> The most devastating thing I saw was a small child, a skeleton
> child, sucking the breast of her dead mother. I vomited. I then
> decided to bring some foreign journalists to the area so that
> they could break to the world the news of what was happening
> in Somalia.

Even veterans of conflict and famine, such as the aid worker Tony Vaux, were deeply affected by what they saw: 'This is the most distressing experience of all my travels for Oxfam over twenty years including Ethiopia in 1984. Somalia is a disaster of terrible proportions. The human suffering is quite unbelievable.'

Once images of the catastrophe hit television screens across the world, international public pressure mounted for something to be done. But this was an extremely difficult, dangerous and unusual situation; Somalia was a country without government, affected by vicious, unpredictable and widespread violence. It was almost impossible to find a way of delivering humanitarian assistance to those who needed it most. The situation was so bad that aid ships were being shot at even before they reached land.

Intervention

About eighteen months after Mogadishu imploded, the United Nations Security Council authorized in April 1992 the deployment of some three thousand peacekeepers to Somalia, in a mission known as UNOSOM. It became clear almost immediately that something far more ambitious was needed. The outgoing US president, George Bush, took the lead, proposing that American troops should lead a much larger UN operation to ensure the safe delivery of humanitarian supplies to the starving, displaced and wounded people of Somalia. On 3 December 1992, for the first time in its history, the Security Council approved unilateral UN intervention with the use of offensive military force in a sovereign state. UNOSOM was replaced by UNITAF. Early the next year 'Operation Restore Hope' was launched; some six hundred members of the foreign media flew into Somalia to record the surreal scenes of bewildered US forces landing on the beaches of Mogadishu at night, blinking into the cameras as they first set foot in the country they had come to 'save'. More than 25,000 American troops were involved in the operation.

'Operation Restore Hope' had some initial success in ensuring aid convoys reached their destinations without being attacked and pillaged by clan militias. But neither the UN nor the USA fully understood the complexity of the situation on the ground, and things soon started to go badly wrong. By now, the mission had become the largest UN operation in the world; known as UNOSOM II, it had some 30,000 personnel, and cost approximately US$1.5 billion a year.

Some Somali factions started to perceive the armed foreign peacekeepers as if they were members of a rival clan, which could only be dealt with violently, especially when they behaved in what appeared to be a provocative way. This was the case in June 1993 when more than twenty Pakistani peacekeepers were killed as they attempted to carry out an inspection of weapons belonging to

General Aideed's fighters. The killing of the Pakistanis was met with a ferocious reaction from the commander of 'Operation Restore Hope', the American admiral Jonathan Howe, who, to all intents and purposes, declared war on General Aideed, putting a US$20,000 bounty on his head. General Aideed lived up to his nickname, which meant 'he who doesn't take offence lying down', by announcing that he would return the compliment by paying US$20,000 to anybody who brought him the actual head of Admiral Howe, or 'Animal' Howe as he was known by many in Somalia.

US forces became increasingly aggressive, stopping and searching Somalis in the streets and raiding Bakara market, where weapons and ammunition were sold alongside cloth, household goods, meat and vegetables. Bakara market, the largest in Mogadishu, must be one of the most heavily targeted shopping areas on earth. It has been raided and shelled for years; during the mid- to late 2000s, Somali government forces and African Union peacekeepers regularly attacked Bakara as it was considered to be a haven for al-Shabaab, and an important source of revenue for the movement.

The conflict between General Aideed and the American military came to a head in October 1993 in what is now known as the 'First Battle of Mogadishu' or 'Black Hawk Down'. Two American Black Hawk helicopters were shot down in the streets of the city. During a massive military operation to rescue the crew, eighteen US servicemen were killed, the bodies of some dragged through the streets. The exact number of Somalis killed during the intense fighting is unknown; estimates put it in the hundreds. This incident, which brought back memories of Vietnam, was too much for the USA. The new president, Bill Clinton, ordered his troops home; most had left by the following year.

A depleted and demoralized UN peacekeeping operation struggled on but was virtually ineffective. When I visited

Mogadishu in 1994, the 'blue helmets' were all but invisible outside UN bases. I saw a few peacekeepers cowering behind sandbags at checkpoints in the city, but by this time they had essentially been defeated by the people they had originally come to save. The remaining peacekeepers soon departed, largely abandoning Somalia to its own fate.

The US/UN military intervention of the 1990s was probably the most dramatic example of 'getting Somalia wrong'. It represented the archetypal wrong-headed exercise in building a state with foreign soldiers and good intentions; the more recent examples of Iraq and Afghanistan suggest lessons from this fiasco still have not been learned. Bradbury outlines how foreign policy failures in Somalia had repercussions for the next major African disaster, the Rwandan genocide of 1994:

> For President Bush, buoyed by the allied victory in the Gulf, the military and humanitarian operation provided an opportunity for the US to demonstrate its role of global policeman in the 'new world order' ... The US Permanent Representative to the UN Madeleine Albright announced the intervention was 'aimed at nothing less than the restoration of an entire community as a proud, functioning and viable member of the community of nations' ... UNOSOM was a poorly considered, poorly informed and poorly managed operation that had a profound effect on Somalia and on international responses to other crises. Bush's vision of a new world order was buried on the streets of Mogadishu and the reluctance of the US to respond to the genocide of Rwanda was a direct consequence of this.[18]

It is ironic that while General Aideed was fighting the Americans and the UN, members of his Habr Gedir clan were making good money out of 'the enemy' and probably funnelling some of the international funds into Aideed's war chest. Some worked as administrators and translators for UNOSOM, and it is likely they passed some of the information about the peacekeeping operation to Aideed's faction.

As in many conflict situations, humanitarian workers in Somalia often had to make 'deals with the devil' in order to do their work. They rented homes and offices from wealthy businessmen, some of whom financed the warlords. In hospitals, fighters often insisted they receive medical treatment before civilians, using their guns to make sure their demands were met. Aid organizations paid thousands of dollars to Somali gunmen to protect their personnel, property, vehicles and humanitarian supplies. The faction that controlled the port made a fortune by taxing aid shipments and diverting some of the humanitarian deliveries for sale for their own profit or to distribute to their supporters and fighters. Bradbury describes the negative unintended consequences of the international intervention:

> Much has now been written on the way in which international humanitarian responses can become embroiled in wars, as a focus for violent appropriation, fuelling a war economy or sustaining predatory structures. In the early 1990s Somalia provided a classic case study. UNOSOM's huge intervention in the south entrenched the predatory warlord structures, spawned a new class of entrepreneurs and perpetuated Mogadishu as a locus of conflict.[19]

This situation has continued throughout the years of conflict. A 2010 report by a UN monitoring group said up to half of all food aid to Somalia was being diverted to corrupt contractors and Islamist militants.[20] Although the UN World Food Programme initially denied the allegations, it announced it would stop using the three Somali contractors named in the report.

'Virtual' government

After the debacle of UNOSOM, foreign powers adopted an entirely different approach, and kept themselves at a distance from Somalia. Apart from the involvement of a few UN agencies and other non-governmental organizations the country was pretty much left to itself. Violence continued, central government remained absent, and those who could fled the country unless they were fighting or making good money from activities that flourished in the lawless environment.

The era of direct intervention was over; it was now time for a long succession of internationally sponsored peace conferences, held a safe distance away in the neighbouring countries of Ethiopia, Kenya and Djibouti. These conferences, with hundreds of delegates representing clans, political parties and other interest groups, dragged on for months or sometimes even years. They were fantastically expensive, costing the United Nations, the African Union, the European Union and others millions of dollars. Although these meetings failed to bring peace to Somalia, they may have helped to assuage a feeling of guilt among outsiders; foreign powers could be seen to be 'doing something' about Somalia without the risk of much direct involvement in the country itself.

These national reconciliation conferences became a major industry for many of the Somali delegates, some of whom were selected naively and arbitrarily by the UN and other bodies. They could stay in hotels and eat good food, all at someone else's expense. Most important of all, they could stay outside Somalia, far away from the bloodshed and danger. They had a vested interest in dragging the meetings out for as long as possible; the Kenyan authorities became so desperate during one marathon conference that lasted for more than two years that they organized a 'farewell party' for the delegates as a polite way of telling them it was time to go home.

One reason why the conferences were doomed to failure was

that, even if they gave lip-service to federalism, they tended to concentrate on the formation of a central government based in Mogadishu. A number of 'transitional' governments were formed during the conferences but they were unable to function effectively in Somalia. The administration headed by President Abdullahi Yusuf in 2005 could not even go to Mogadishu, so deep was the enmity towards him. His government was initially based in the town of Jowhar, about ninety kilometres from Mogadishu. It then had to move even farther away, to the southern town of Baidoa, after Abdullahi Yusuf fell out with one of Jowhar's powerful warlords.

Even though these transitional administrations were internationally recognized as the legitimate authorities in Somalia, they were in reality no more than 'virtual' governments because they controlled hardly anything. For example, the prime minister of one of these administrations, Omar Abdirashid Ali Sharmarke, assured me in 2009 that he would eliminate piracy within the next two years. But, as his government had no authority in the parts of Somalia where the pirates operated, his promise was empty.

Even more surreal is the presence in hotels in the Kenyan capital, Nairobi, of a number of self-declared 'presidents' of different parts of Somalia. In October 2010, I sat in amazement in the lobby of the Andalus Hotel in the predominantly Somali district of Eastleigh as delegations from various Somali 'governments' swept past me, dressed in smart suits with their territories' 'flags' pinned to their lapels. Many of the 'cabinet members' of these self-declared governments came from the Somali diaspora in Europe and the United States. Some had never been to the areas they claimed to govern. A number of 'real' Somali MPs, who are supposed to work in the parliament in Mogadishu, spend far more time in Nairobi than in Somalia, living in peace instead of braving the daily bullets and mortar shells.

Alternative authority

While the reconciliation conferences dragged on and a succession of transitional governments were established, alternative forms of authority were emerging in Somalia. As will be discussed further in Chapter 4, some regions formed their own administrations, including the self-declared republic of Somaliland and the semi-autonomous region of Puntland. Others experienced the development of more localized forms of law and order, as happened in some parts of Mogadishu and surrounding areas where sharia courts linked to different clans and sub-clans had been providing a degree of justice since the 1990s. In the absence of any effective central government, the courts' authority started to grow. They came together in 2006 to form the Union of Islamic Courts but were driven out after only six months in power in a US-backed Ethiopian invasion.

Several UIC leaders either went into exile in Eritrea, setting up with other opposition figures the Alliance for the Re-liberation of Somalia. Others, including members of the courts' militia, melted into the bush in southern Somalia, near the border with Kenya, re-emerging as the Islamist movement al-Shabaab, which means 'The Youth' in Arabic. This was a far more radical group, which has come to represent a serious international threat. In some ways, US-led policy towards the UIC created the very thing it aimed to destroy; its actions helped to radicalize the movement. By the late 2000s, al-Shabaab and other religious militias controlled large parts of southern and central Somalia, while the internationally recognized government was confined to a few districts of the capital, Mogadishu. Foreign fighters joined the campaign and the movement started to export violence. In July 2010, two al-Shabaab suicide bombers killed seventy-four people as they watched the football World Cup final in the Ugandan capital Kampala.

The two decades of international efforts to resolve the crisis in Somalia have achieved very little, and have in some instances backfired significantly. The territory has lurched from one form of conflict to another, with violence remaining one of the few constants in many people's lives. This is not the whole picture. Parts of Somali territory have been peaceful, but a generation has grown up knowing nothing but conflict, especially in south-central Somalia. When I speak to people living in Mogadishu or other places affected by years of fighting, the first thing they talk about is the noise, the sound of gunfire and shelling; when I speak to Somalis who have come away from these areas, for a short break in Hargeisa, Nairobi or London, the first thing they talk about is how good it is to get away from the sounds of bullets, rockets and mortars.

One person in Mogadishu to whom I speak almost every day is the BBC reporter Mohamed Moalimuu. After we greet each other, he gives me a rundown of what has happened that day. In a businesslike way, he informs me how many people have been killed, the number of wounded, whether any of them are children or pregnant women. He tells me who started the fighting, how heavy it is, and for precisely how many hours and minutes it has lasted, sometimes holding the phone up so I can hear the gunfire and pounding of shells. He is always calm, measured and gracious. But one day he called me at home, sounding shaken and upset. Instead of the usual efficient few minutes, he spent a long time talking to me. He described how he had been to see a group of people who had been forced out of their homes by the authorities, who then demolished their properties, saying they had been used as al-Shabaab hideouts. He said he had found the families gathered in an open area, living without shelter on the bare earth. There he had seen a little boy. What was upsetting Moalimuu so much was that this boy had fashioned a gun out of a stick and was playing with it. Somehow this, something little boys do all over the world, upset him more deeply than the awful consequences of violence he sees nearly every day. When I went

3 Displaced boy in Mogadishu plays with a gun made from a stick (Mohamed Moalimuu)

to work the next day, I found an email from Moalimuu with a photo attached. I opened it and saw a little boy dressed in red playing with his pretend gun in the sand.

The US-based Somali academic Said S. Samatar believes the years of violence have changed the mind-set and culture of his people. Writing in 2010, he painted a picture of a world gone mad:

> What is unprecedented in the new catastrophic cataclysm of Somalia's continuing civil strife concerns a universal explosion of purposeless violence, a colossal mass hysteria which led to a wholesale unravelling of traditional normative values that mediated the rules of violence through time-tested sanctions of checks and balances. The consequences of this breakdown of the traditional regulators of inter-clan discourse [are] patently a traumatised deranged society, in which men and women have taken to blindly falling on one another, flailing amorphously, hacking away at one another, or rather indiscriminately

machine-gunning everything that moves in a dazed hysteria reminiscent of a kind of mad dance that could only have been drawn from the pages of a Dostoevsky novel ... As I write, on average, in the capital city of Mogadishu, thirty to forty people are killed daily with no one knowing who targeted them or why. The killing is all! If today a stranger with a loudspeaker descended from the sky and inquired of the denizens of Mogadishu: 'Why are you shooting?' the answer would undoubtedly resound back: 'Because this is our way of life.' No wonder Somalia is said to represent for African states a cautionary tale of where not to go.[21]

In many ways, the example of Somalia is also a cautionary tale of how 'not to do it' in terms of foreign policy or humanitarian intervention. This brief overview of the country's history has shown how problems have recurred since colonial times, and how attempts to resolve them have often repeated similar mistakes time and again throughout the decades. Observations by British colonial officials are almost as relevant today as they were in the early years of the twentieth century. Of course, the problems have manifested themselves in different ways during different periods of Somali history, but they share some fundamental similarities which should not be ignored.

Internal and external efforts to bring peace to Somalia, and to help those in need, have often backfired. Despite these failures, those trying to find solutions seem trapped in a recurring nightmare of 'peace conferences' and 'transitional administrations'. Too many people have ignored the fact that the years without effective authority, peace and stability have led to some fascinating and successful home-grown experiments in how to live without a state; these examples could serve as useful lessons and triggers for ideas of how to tackle the situation in other parts of Somalia, and indeed other parts of the world. The years of instability and lack of effective government have also spawned many different breeds of violent groups, the latest of which are often Islamist in character. The next chapter will trace the development of violent Islamism in Somalia. It will show that the al-Qaeda-linked group al-Shabaab, and other militant Islamist organizations, did not spring completely out of the blue, but have roots that can be traced back for several decades.

3 | ISLAMISM

Somalia in 2011: the north-west has gone its own way and functioned as the relatively successful self-declared republic of Somaliland for the past twenty years; other parts of northern Somalia have not severed ties so completely, but they have their own administrations and operate as semi-autonomous units; parts of the capital, Mogadishu, are controlled by the transitional government, which depends for its survival on the backing of African Union troops from Uganda and Burundi; many other parts of central and southern Somalia are controlled by the Islamist al-Shabaab militia, which professes allegiance to al-Qaeda and has imposed draconian rules that have forced people to profoundly alter their way of life. Women have to wear thick, heavy robes and veils over their faces, men have their heads shaved with pieces of broken glass if their hair is too long,[1] mobile phones are smashed if they play musical ring tones, and people accused of adultery have been buried in the sand and stoned to death by members of the public.

The areas controlled by al-Shabaab are not united under a strong, centralized Islamist administration; the experience of each town and village varies according to which group of militants control it at which particular time. This man, who did not want to give his name, spoke from the al-Shabaab-controlled town of Jowhar, about ninety kilometres north of Mogadishu:

> The first and most important thing I would like to say about
> life in Jowhar is that there is security in the town. There are
> no bandits or robbers because al-Shabaab would cut off their

hands or worse if it caught them. The threat of this kind of punishment really works.

The good security situation means people are free to move around in Jowhar; they can go wherever they want, even in the middle of the night. This is impossible in the parts of southern and central Somalia not under the control of the Islamist militias.

But freedom of movement is the only type of freedom we have. There is no freedom of speech. People cannot say what they want, and they certainly cannot complain about al-Shabaab because there are spies everywhere. If someone speaks out against the Islamists, he or she is sure to get a threatening phone call from al-Shabaab. People have been executed after being accused of spying for the transitional government, the Ethiopians or the Americans. There is a kind of mind control going on in this town.

We have almost no form of entertainment left in Jowhar. It is as if al-Shabaab does not want us to enjoy anything. We are not allowed to play music and we are forbidden from watching films in the video parlours, which used to be one of our most popular forms of amusement. We are allowed to watch certain Islamic television stations inside our houses but this is very isolating and lonely.

One of the things young people in Jowhar used to love doing was going to the video halls to watch football matches. Many of them have now completely lost interest in sport because watching football on television at home alone is no fun at all.

The villages in our region used to have football tournaments. It was such fun going to watch the games. But these matches have been forbidden, even though boys are permitted to play informal games of football. Al-Shabaab is encouraging people to have bow and arrow shooting competitions. I think this is because it trains the young to develop a sharp eye for shooting and to become good fighters.

There are still schools in Jowhar but the situation has become very difficult. Boys and girls are segregated, and al-Shabaab militants often come to preach in the schools. Once or twice a week, they speak to the children about the importance of jihad. This has caused friction between the generations because children come home from school shouting about how wonderful it is to fight jihad; they quarrel with their parents and refuse to listen to them when they say violence is a bad thing.

Al-Shabaab has enforced a new kind of fashion in Jowhar. Women are not allowed to go outside without covering their faces. They have to wear loose and heavy robes; sometimes you see their eyes peeking out, other times you see nothing. It's impossible to tell if a woman is young, middle-aged or old. Even the nomadic women have to wear these terrible clothes when they come to sell milk in the town and surrounding villages.

The men have not escaped either. The militants say we have to grow long beards, and we are forbidden from wearing long trousers. Our ankles have to be exposed.

It's easy to spot the al-Shabaab fighters in Jowhar. They dress in the style of the Taliban. They wear shalwar kameez – long shirts with short trousers, both in the same colour. On top, they wear military jackets, and often have their heads wrapped in Palestinian-style scarves. Some of them carry the black flag of al-Shabaab.

Al-Shabaab does not have a big presence in Jowhar because most of its supporters are out fighting in other parts of the country. About forty to fifty al-Shabaab soldiers patrol our town, but this is enough because they have so many spies working for them. (Jowhar resident, March 2011)

Origins

Many have greeted with surprise what has often been portrayed as the sudden explosion of violent Islamism in Somalia and the opening up of a new front for al-Qaeda. Although militant Islamist groups now wield an unprecedented degree of influence, especially in terms of their control of such large parts of the country, political Islam, including the advocacy of violence to achieve its aims, is not new to Somalia. It can be traced back more than a hundred years, and there is a certain logic to its development. History can be seen repeating itself time and again; Islamist groups come and go, their names change, but the same people and ideologies keep cropping up.

Although it was in no way inevitable that by 2011 large parts of Somalia would be under the sway of an extremist Islamist militia, the rise of al-Shabaab did not occur in a vacuum. But why has this group succeeded in gaining such significant amounts of territory and imposing its beliefs on people when other Islamist groups have failed to do so in the past? Is it because Somalia has been without central authority for so many years? Or is it because al-Qaeda is a globalized phenomenon, ever present on the Internet, inspiring violent radical Islamism in many different parts of the world, and instantly linking disaffected members of the Somali diaspora and other sympathizers with jihadi elements at home?

Before tracing the development of Islamist groups in Somalia, it is important to point out that most Somalis, although almost all are Muslims, do not practise or support militant Islamism. They have their own distinct ways of doing things in terms of religion, as they do in so many other areas of their lives. They have been Muslims for centuries, and have generally practised a fairly tolerant and moderate type of Sunni Islam, respecting different forms of religious observance. Somalis have traditionally venerated Sufi saints and belong to three main Sufi brotherhoods,

4 Al-Shabaab fighters in Mogadishu (Mohamed Moalimuu)

the *Qadiriya*, *Ahmediya* and *Salihiya*. As Lewis argues, Somalis have emphasized the parts of Islam that suit them best: 'Sufi theosophy – as opposed to the Sharia – is in its basic principles suited to Somali society. These principles have been firmly assimilated while what in the Sharia is inapplicable to a clan society has been largely ignored.'[2]

There are, however, precedents for violent political Islam in Somalia. One of the earliest and most well-known examples is Seyyid Mohamed Abdulle Hassan's jihad against colonial forces in the early years of the twentieth century. Even though his mission ultimately failed, the Seyyid's poetry and ideals have continued to inspire Somalis, partly because the marriage of nationalism with religion has remained relevant. The Seyyid's jihad has served as a model for other violent religious movements in Somalia, some of which have been motivated by a similar agenda: to rid the country of outside influence and to establish a 'Greater Somalia'.

The powerful Islamist leader Sheikh Hassan Dahir Aweys, who has played a prominent role in violent Somali religious groups since the 1990s, has in many ways been portrayed by the Western media as a modern-day 'Mad Mullah' with his richly hennaed red beard and rousing politico-religious rhetoric.

Islam continued to play an important role in people's political consciousness in the years leading up to and immediately following independence in 1960. The Islamic faith had for so long been such a key part of the Somali identity that it was in many ways inevitable that it would play a role in the formation of the newly independent, modernizing Somali state. This was an exciting, heady time in Africa; people were breaking free from their colonial past, exploring new ideas in politics, religion and other areas of their lives. Somalis picked up fresh ideas about political Islam from the nearby Arab world; many studied there and were exposed to and influenced by groups such as the Muslim Brotherhood in Egypt.

Siad Barre's coup in 1969 and the subsequent introduction of 'scientific socialism' crushed much of the dynamism and free thinking of the post-independence years. Religion was not immune from this; the turning point came in 1975 when religious leaders voiced strong opposition to the promulgation of new and controversial family legislation, which, among other things, gave more rights to women. The authorities responded to the criticism by executing ten of the most vocal clerics and imprisoning dozens of others.

The killing of the clerics drove some religious groups underground or overseas; religion had by now become a potential form of resistance to Siad Barre. It is ironic that the ideals of some of the religious opposition groups formed abroad echoed closely some of the central tenets of Siad Barre's brand of socialism. A report published by the Norwegian Institute for Urban and Regional Research (NIBR) describes how the Somali group al-Islah, which was founded in Saudi Arabia in 1978, 'showed outright contempt for clan-based politics, and strongly maintained that Islam transcended clans'.[3]

After the fall of Siad Barre and the subsequent collapse of the Somali state, there was an explosion of religious groups in the country. The International Crisis Group describes how 'a bewildering array of Islamic associations suddenly emerged, each purporting to represent a discrete religious doctrine. Their common denominator was the desire for an "authentic" form of Islamic governance in Somalia.'[4] However, most of the powerful groups in the 1990s were run on a clan basis. This was the era of warlordism in Somalia; religion would have to wait its turn. It was not until the twenty-first century that religious groups became dominant players in the conflict. Perhaps they had to wait for the events of 9/11 and the emergence of al-Qaeda as a global role model, as well as the rise of the Internet, mobile phones and other sophisticated forms of communication that could influence, inspire and bring together people with jihadist ambitions.

Al-Itihaad

The most powerful religious group to emerge in Somalia in the early 1990s was al-Itihaad al-Islamiya. It was created by the merger of a number of regional organizations that followed the strict Saudi Wahhabi form of Islam, very different from mainstream Somali religious practices. Al-Itihaad had become defunct by the mid-2000s, but it was in many ways a precursor to al-Shabaab and other extremist groups, including Hizbul Islam, which in 2011 was defeated by al-Shabaab and absorbed into it.

Some of al-Itihaad's members went on to become powerful leaders of the Union of Islamic Courts, al-Shabaab and other groups. They include the man who at the time of writing was generally regarded as the leader of al-Shabaab, Ahmed Abdi Godane, also known as Abu Zubair, and another central figure in the movement, Hassan Turki. The former leader of al-Itihaad, Sheikh Hassan Dahir Aweys, remains a key figure in the Somali Islamist movement, and is in a sense its spiritual head. His role is in some ways similar to that of Sudan's Dr Hassan al-Turabi, who was the spiritual mastermind of the government's 'permanent Islamic revolution'.

Al-Shabaab is in many ways a continuation of al-Itihaad in terms of the ideas it espouses: both groups insisted religion could not be separated from politics and ridiculed Somalia's Sufi orders as un-Islamic. Al-Shabaab is so opposed to Sufi practices that it has desecrated several Sufi graves, including the tombs of important saints.

Al-Itihaad initially established an Islamist 'emirate' near the port of Bossasso in north-eastern Somalia, which served as a base and training facility for about a thousand fighters. It was driven out of the region and in 1992 set up base in the town of Luq in southern Somalia's Gedo region, near the border with Ethiopia. Some al-Itihaad fighters crossed the border into eastern Ethiopia, where they joined the rebel Ogaden National Liberation Front, which has for years been fighting for the rights of Ethiopia's ethnic Somali population. The International Crisis Group explains how, like other religious groups, al-Itihaad filled the vacuum left after the collapse of central authority: 'Over the next few years it emerged as the pre-eminent military and political force in Gedo, largely thanks to the order and discipline it represented in an otherwise lawless and chaotic environment.'[5]

The movement was also similar to al-Shabaab in the type of laws it imposed. The Somalia expert Ken Menkhaus describes how in its Luq 'emirate' the 'consumption of the mild narcotic leaf *qat*, a popular habit, was forbidden, as was the cultivation of tobacco. Veiling was enforced on women.'[6]

As with the Union of Islamic Courts, the downfall of al-Itihaad came about when it turned its attention to the Somali-dominated parts of Ethiopia. In the mid-1990s, it started to agitate for the liberation of the region and carried out grenade attacks in Ethiopia's eastern town of Dire Dawa and the capital, Addis Ababa, killing several people. In response, Ethiopia carried out aerial raids on Luq, smashing al-Itihaad as an effective movement.

Al-Itihaad also caught the attention of the United States; a few days after the bombing of the Twin Towers in September 2001, George Bush issued an Executive Order blocking the assets of twenty-seven organizations and individuals he said were linked to terrorism. Al-Itihaad was number ten on the list.

Union of Islamic Courts

Alternative systems of dispensing law and order have been used in Somalia during the long years of warlordism and inter-clan conflict. The existence of a deeply ingrained traditional legal system, especially among the nomads, meant that the population was relatively well suited to coping with the progressive collapse of the state.

Other systems were also developing to fill the vacuum; in some parts of the country, sharia courts emerged as key providers of justice and order. Their authority was initially limited to very small areas; for example, in the capital Mogadishu, each court's jurisdiction extended to just a few city blocks. Some emerged shortly after the fall of Siad Barre, such as the courts in the parts of north Mogadishu controlled by the clan leader Ali Mahdi Mohamed. From the early 1990s, they provided some form of legal system in the area, carrying out amputations and other sharia punishments.

At the outset, the courts represented little more than a loosely defined group of independent, discrete units, each one taking responsibility for establishing a degree of order within its very limited area of influence. As the years went by, and nothing emerged to take their place, the authority of the courts began to grow, and was often welcomed by a population weary of banditry and warlords.

The courts started to represent an alternative power system when they united to face a common enemy, the US-backed Alliance for the Restoration of Peace and Counter-Terrorism, which was formed by a group of warlords in 2006. In the post-9/11 world, the 'Alliance' found it easy to present the sharia courts to the USA and its allies as a serious 'terrorist' threat and a potential breeding ground for Islamist extremists. It is possible that if this 'anti-terror' alliance had never been formed and had not been given so much credibility by the USA, the courts would never have united, remaining instead as a largely unrelated group of small bodies serving the needs of discrete sections of Somalia's population. It is only when they were faced with a hostile alliance of warlords that the courts stopped being a loose federation and united into a more homogeneous body, with a clearer authority structure.

Much to the surprise of the outside world, the UIC militarily defeated the warlords' alliance in Mogadishu, and, for the latter half of 2006, controlled significant parts of southern and central Somalia. The Somalia expert Roland Marchal argues that 'the victory of the courts in Mogadishu meant the end of the faction as a form for organizing Somali political life, a role it had held since 1991 ... This victory also signalled the arrival of a new generation of political figures.' Marchal highlights what he describes as the 'extraordinarily complex' relationship between the sharia courts and the clans: 'In a way, the courts themselves are clan institutions ... the courts have very diverse ties to the clans. In some instances, their influence is limited; in others, the ties are deep and longstanding.'[7]

For the brief six months it was in power, life under the UIC was, for many Somalis, safer than it had been for the past sixteen years. Unlike the warlords, the foreign peacekeepers and the long succession of transitional governments, the UIC managed to make life less dangerous. The period of UIC control has been romanticized, but there is no doubt that people could, for the first time in years, walk the streets without fear.

In their paper *The Rise and Fall of Mogadishu's Islamic Courts*, Cedric Barnes and Harun Hassan describe the dramatic improvements in the city:

> The courts achieved the unthinkable, uniting Mogadishu for the first time in sixteen years, and re-establishing peace and security. The courts undertook significant and highly symbolic public actions. Road-blocks were removed and even the ubiquitous piles of rubbish that had blighted the city for a decade or more were cleared. The main Mogadishu airport and seaport were reopened and rehabilitated for the first time in a decade. Squatters were made to vacate government buildings, illegal land grabs were halted, and special courts were opened to deal with the myriad claims for the restitution of property.[8]

The population paid a price for peace. Bloody sharia punishments were carried out, *qat* was banned, women had to cover themselves, and people were not allowed to watch films in public video halls. But as people who lived under the UIC described, the violence and banditry that had blighted their lives for one and a half decades were dramatically reduced:

> When the UIC came into the country they made safety and peace for the citizens a priority. They made sure that every robber gave up his gun, all the video spots were closed, every *qat* seller stopped selling poison to people, everything was calm and quiet. And it was really what the people wanted, after living in war for sixteen years. It was like Allah answered all our prayers.[9]

In the areas it controlled, the UIC was more successful than any of the other post-Barre experiments in addressing security and other concerns. Because the courts emerged from a grassroots level to perform some of the key functions of government in a stateless society, they were increasingly viewed as legitimate authorities by the communities they served.

The most significant contribution of the Islamic courts was the way in which they ensured basic law and order, including the enforcement of contracts, which made it possible to have commercial and civil life. One of the functions of Islam is that it provides an off-the-shelf, culturally validated code for many aspects of social, economic and political life, which allows for a form of public order and administration in the absence of a state.

Some of the UIC's policies attracted criticism because of their economic consequences; the more it became like a proper 'government', the more unpopular it became. The banning of *qat*, for instance, had serious repercussions, not only for the many Somalis who made a living from selling the leaves, but for the growers and exporters in Kenya and Ethiopia. The UIC also banned charcoal exports because it said burning trees to make charcoal was bad for the environment. This alienated those whose livelihoods depended on making and selling charcoal, and those who relied on it for cooking. The UIC provoked public protests in October 2006 when it introduced significant tax increases; the population had become used to a more anarchic system whereby they paid off warlords and other militias, but did not have their incomes regulated by any central authority.

As the courts gained power, they were seized upon by the politically ambitious, principally Sheikh Hassan Dahir Aweys, the former leader of al-Itihaad, and an active promoter of the interests of the Ayr sub-clan. With the help of his fellow Ayr member and Afghan-trained lieutenant, Adan Hashi Ayro, who transformed the court militias into the highly disciplined al-Shabaab army, Aweys sidelined moderate elements in the UIC and alienated

many non-Ayr clan members. Ayro, like Aweys, had been involved with violent Islamist movements for some years, fighting
in north-eastern Somalia and the Somali region of Ethiopia in
the 1990s. He received military training in Afghanistan at least
twice, and, according to the US-based Jamestown Foundation,
met Osama bin Laden when he was there. Ayro was killed by a
US Tomahawk cruise missile in Somalia in May 2008, and almost
instantly elevated to the position of a heroic martyr, galvaniz-
ing al-Shabaab fighters to intensify their activities. In a video
released posthumously, Ayro talks about the glory of dying for
the cause: 'Most of us in al-Shabaab feel that our morale and
spirits will be lifted with each martyrdom in our ranks … It is
a great honour to become a martyr. We can attain great success
by seeking martyrdom and by shoving sand into the mouths of
infidels and their collaborating hypocrites.'

Aweys was keen to spread his beliefs beyond Somalia's borders,
especially in Ethiopia. In mid-December 2006, the UIC declared
a jihad against Ethiopia; by doing so it signed its own death
warrant. The declaration gave Ethiopia's prime minister, Meles
Zenawi, the excuse he needed to go to war; he was supported
by the United States, which was keen to rid Somalia of the UIC.
This arrangement suited the USA because Ethiopia could fight on
its behalf, and there was no need for a repeat of the disastrous
US intervention of the early 1990s.

On Christmas Day 2006 Ethiopian fighter jets bombarded
Mogadishu's air and sea ports. The UIC had no hope of standing
up to Ethiopia's giant military machine, especially its air power
and the surveillance assistance it received from the USA. Just
a week later, on New Year's Day 2007, the UIC abandoned its
last urban stronghold, the southern port city of Kismayo. Most
of its leadership fled to Eritrea, and its fighters disappeared into
impenetrable bush near the Kenyan border.

Although Ethiopia represented the 'public face' of the

Christmas Day invasion, the USA was also directly involved. On 9 January, a huge American AC-130 gunship dropped bombs on to the south-eastern tip of Somalia. The stated goal was the elimination of an al-Qaeda cell; as well as being opposed to what it saw as the extremist threat posed by the UIC, the USA believed the lawless situation in Somalia made it an ideal safe haven for senior al-Qaeda operatives. A principal target was Fazul Abdullah Mohamed, a Comorean national with a Kenyan passport, whom the USA accused of being behind the 1998 bombings of its embassies in Nairobi and Dar es Salaam, and the 2002 attacks on a Mombasa hotel and an Israeli airliner. He was eventually killed in Mogadishu in June 2011 in a shoot-out involving government troops; documents found on his body suggested he was planning a series of attacks in Britain, including one on the prestigious Eton College.

Shortly after the Ethiopian invasion, Somalia's defence minister, Colonel Barre Aden Shire, announced the total defeat of the Islamists. With the Kenyan border sealed, US warships patrolling the coast and heavily armed Ethiopian and transitional government troops advancing from the north, he said they had little choice but 'to drown in the sea or to fight and die'. Once the American air raids began, it was not only the Islamists who were killed, but dozens of nomads, and their livestock. This provoked strong anti-US sentiments; as one Somali put it, 'the Americans are beating the dead'.

The UIC leaders described their flight from Mogadishu as a 'tactical withdrawal', saying an 'Iraqi-style insurgency' would follow. Such a strategy was encouraged by radical Islamists elsewhere in the world, some of whom had adopted UIC militiamen as their fellow jihadists. In an audio recording from al-Qaeda's second-in-command at the time, Ayman al-Zawahiri, Muslims were called upon to join Somalis in 'launching ambushes, land mines, raids and suicidal combats' against 'the crusader invading

Ethiopian forces' and to 'consume them as the lions eat their prey'.

The UIC's miscalculated declaration of jihad against Ethiopia led to its military defeat, but it had already won the battle for hearts and minds. For most Somalis, the presence of Ethiopian troops on their soil, and American gunships in their skies, was intolerable. On 6 January, just a few days after the UIC was driven out of Mogadishu, Somalis in the capital staged rowdy demonstrations against the Ethiopians. Three protesters were shot dead. By 7 January, the protests had spread to the town of Belet Huen, closer to the Ethiopian border. Insecurity increased as soon as the UIC left Mogadishu. People's immediate priority was self-protection. They ignored the incoming transitional federal government's call for disarmament; the air was filled with gunshots as people tested new weapons bought in the markets. In the words of one Mogadishu resident, 'We are back to square one, back to 1991', referring to the violent anarchy that followed the fall of President Siad Barre.

The Ethiopian occupation and the US airstrikes did not succeed in eliminating Islamism from Somalia. Quite the opposite; the UIC re-emerged in a far more dangerous form as al-Shabaab, which took over large parts of central and southern Somalia, including most of Mogadishu. In many areas, clan militias were replaced by religious armies, including al-Shabaab, Hizbul Islam and the Sufi group Ahlu Sunna Wa Jamaa, which fought on the side of the transitional government against the radical Islamist movements.

Al-Shabaab

Al-Shabaab grew from being a small militia associated with a group of sharia courts into Somalia's most powerful and effective Islamist movement. As described in the opening pages of this chapter, it imposed its way of life on many parts of the country.

Al-Shabaab has global recognition; it was put on the US list of foreign terrorist organizations in 2008, and banned by the UK in 2010. Al-Shabaab has joined the al-Qaeda franchise, saying for the first time in 2010 that its 'jihad in the Horn of Africa must be combined with the international jihad led by the al-Qaeda network'.[10]

As al-Shabaab is such a secretive movement it is difficult to ascertain exactly what it is fighting for and who its leaders are. Both its ideology and its leadership appear to change fairly regularly, and the movement should not be seen as entirely homogeneous. A UN Security Report released in 2010 described the movement as: 'a sprawling coalition of jihadists, business interests and clan militias, which has suffered serious internal frictions over such issues as the role of foreign fighters, the use of suicide bombers and desirability of political dialogue'.[11]

Al-Shabaab has ideological divisions, with some leaders saying they are fighting for the establishment of an Islamic republic within Somalia's current borders, some that they want to establish the 'Islamic Republic of Greater Somalia', and others that they want to take the jihad far beyond 'Greater Somalia', creating a giant Islamic state stretching down into East Africa and up towards Egypt. At times, al-Shabaab becomes even more ambitious; in May 2009 the movement's leader, Sheikh Ahmed Abdi Godane, declared, 'We will fight and the wars will not end until Islamic sharia is implemented in all continents in the world and until Muslims liberate Jerusalem.'

There are also variations in al-Shabaab's approach to military tactics. It began with hit-and-run attacks, briefly occupying towns and villages, then withdrawing from them to go and fight elsewhere. This spread terror in many parts of Somalia. Al-Shabaab later became an occupying force in some areas, leading to a greater degree of stability and enabling it to impose more rigorously its strict rules and regulations. In August 2011, al-Shabaab

5 Mogadishu after the withdrawal of al-Shabaab, September 2011
(Mohamed Moalimuu)

announced it was withdrawing from the capital, Mogadishu. The
transitional government said this was a victory for its forces,
but in all likelihood the move represented a reversal of tactics
by al-Shabaab, which was at the time weakened by leadership
divisions and the loss of key sources of finance.

One reason why it is so difficult to find out what al-Shabaab
wants is that it is not always easy to find someone to speak to
within the movement, especially because I am a woman and
a Westerner. After several days of speaking to intermediaries,
sending and receiving text messages to and from a variety of
numbers, and making phone calls only to be told to call yet
another number, I secured in March 2011 a telephone appointment with the Islamist leader, Sheikh Hassan Dahir Aweys. The
timing of the appointment was changed at the last minute, and
another succession of phone calls and text messages was required
before I actually spoke to him. When I asked him, with the help

of a translator, what al-Shabaab was fighting for, he gave me an elliptical answer, speaking in a loud and confident voice, occasionally breaking into laughter or expressing outrage at my questions:

> We are fighting for three reasons. Firstly, our country has been invaded. Secondly, we are being prevented from practising our religious beliefs. Thirdly, we are fighting against those who are blocking the interests of our people by preventing them from establishing an Islamic government.
>
> The entity that is now known as the 'government of Somalia' is not a real government; it is a cover-up government, a fake government. They tried to trick people by putting some opposition members into the government, in an effort to diffuse our objectives and principles. But we don't accept this; we will continue to fight this fake institution, and inshallah we will win.
>
> The concept of democracy, which started in Greece, is now being forced down the throats of every nation. I believe Islam is far more international than democracy. Islamic government is what we are seeking to establish here in Somalia instead of the democracy that is being forced upon us.
>
> Everything that has happened in Somalia has been planned by Washington. The Americans will do anything they can to prevent an Islamic government being formed in Somalia.
>
> The first thing we want to do is establish proper Islamic rule within Somalia's current borders. Since one hundred per cent of Somalis are Muslims, they must comply with the correct Islamic principles. The next step in our campaign will come later, and that will require the understanding of our neighbours and the international community.
>
> We share a way of thinking with al-Qaeda, but as our country has been militarized for so long, we don't need any outside help. Al-Shabaab does not have an administrative relationship with al-Qaeda.

Even more difficult than speaking to the leadership of al-Shabaab is speaking to its foot soldiers, many of whom are instructed not to talk to outsiders. In April 2011, I managed to speak to a former al-Shabaab fighter, known as Al Ahzari, who had left the movement and was living in Mogadishu, under the protection of the transitional government:

> I joined al-Shabaab in 2006 because, at that time, I believed it was fighting for the Islamic religion. I was in charge of a unit and we fought all over Somalia: in the south near the border with Kenya, in Mogadishu, in Kismayo, and many other parts of south-central Somalia.
>
> These days, people are not paid to fight for al-Shabaab; they are told they are fighting for the cause of Islam. Even fighters with children who have nothing to eat or drink are not paid – they are told 'Allah will provide'.
>
> Life was difficult in al-Shabaab because all I did was fight. We were asked to fight against African Union peacekeepers who had military vehicles and heavy weaponry. All we had were light weapons like AK-47s. When we complained, we were accused of being hypocrites and dealt with accordingly.
>
> Those who become suicide bombers for al-Shabaab are generally very young. They are trained for about six months; every day they are brainwashed and told they will go to paradise. Some senior al-Shabaab members pretend they are also undergoing training to become suicide bombers; they start weeping and crying that they too want to go on suicide missions but are told by the trainers that others have been selected, that their time will come. They use this as a psychological tactic to mislead the young trainees. Al-Shabaab always has several suicide bombers ready to go – between thirty and seventy at a time.

Al-Shabaab focuses a lot of its attention on indoctrinating the young. As described at the beginning of this chapter, it preaches jihad to children at school. It also employs other more bizarre and macabre techniques to introduce children to violence, and to encourage them to use it.

One particularly extreme example occurred in the southern town of Merca in October 2009 on the day of the execution of two people accused of spying. Al-Shabaab ordered all schools in the town to shut for the day so that children could come and watch the executions. Militants patrolled the town with loudspeakers, instructing people to go to the patch of open ground where the executions were to take place. Most of the people in the crowd were women and children, and they had little choice but to watch the killing of the two 'spies'.

Another incident occurred in the same year in the southern port of Kismayo. During the month of Ramadan, al-Shabaab organized a quiz for young men in the town. Most of the questions related to the Islamic faith. The organizer of the quiz, Abdiweli Mohamed Adam, said the aim of the competition was to stop young men from wasting their time and to focus on important things like defending their territory and their religion.

At the end of Ramadan, hundreds of people attended the prize-giving ceremony for the winners of the quiz. Abdiweli Mohamed Adam described the prizes to the assembled crowd: 'The winner gets an AK-47 rifle – a brand new one – plus two hand grenades, an anti-tank mine and some office equipment, including a computer. Second prize is a second-hand AK-47 and some office supplies. Never in my life have I seen such rewards.' The prizes were passed around the spectators, with al-Shabaab militants encouraging parents to let their children handle the weapons, saying this would help them learn how to fight the enemy.

Another disturbing technique is the distribution of DVDs of Bollywood movies among those training for suicide missions. Impressionable teenagers have been told that these are films of paradise, shot by al-Shabaab militants who are already living in heaven and experiencing all its delights after blowing themselves up in suicide attacks.

I asked Sheikh Hassan Dahir Aweys how he could justify the indoctrination of children and their recruitment into al-Shabaab: 'When it comes to child recruitment, in Islam the age of responsibility is defined as fifteen years old. Any child younger than fifteen years of age does not take part in the fighting. But elderly people and women who want to participate in battles are allowed to do so, because that is allowed in our religion.'

I met some boys who had escaped forced recruitment by al-Shabaab by fleeing across the border to Kenya, where they ended up in Nairobi's Eastleigh district. It was not easy to find them. They were in hiding from the Kenyan police because they had no papers, and were in the country illegally. I was taken far into the backstreets of Eastleigh, to another world where recent arrivals from Somalia shelter in dilapidated buildings. It took time and effort to convince the boys to come out, but eventually they emerged into the black dust of the street, standing among the open drains and mountains of rubbish. They took a while to speak, but once they started they would not stop. A large crowd of Somali boys gathered around us, whooping and shouting in support as the two new arrivals spoke of their hostility to al-Shabaab, the fear never leaving their eyes. The first to talk was Mohamed. He said he was fifteen years old and had fled the town of Baidoa:

> I fled my home town because al-Shabaab fighters there force young people to join them. Boys in Baidoa have only two options; to join al-Shabaab or to flee the areas it controls. The Islamists punish young people who resist them; they slap, beat and arrest them, forcing them to join the militia. Many of my classmates have been forced to join al-Shabaab; they are already fighting for them. I don't have any family or friends in

Kenya, and it is very difficult because the Kenyan police are always hunting us down. But I will survive.

The second boy, perhaps emboldened by Mohamed, gave a long speech against al-Shabaab. His said his name was Abdirahman and that he had come from Mogadishu:

I left because of all the pressure I was coming under from al-Shabaab. The group's scholars came to the parts of town where young people gather and told us we had to join the jihad. They paid some of my friends to join, and indoctrinated others so that they joined for religious reasons. The scholars told us we had to fight because jihad is a religious obligation. Al-Shabaab tried to make us believe that if we didn't join them we were not Muslims. I am always afraid here in Kenya. I am terrified every single minute that I am going to be picked up by the authorities and sent back to Somalia. I have no ID papers, no documents, so they can arrest me at any time. I have seen the police swoop on Eastleigh, rounding up Somalis. When that happens, I run away as fast as I can.

Militant Islamist groups perpetually introduce new rules, each one further suppressing forms of behaviour that are central to the Somali way of life. First, people were forbidden from watching films and football matches in public. Then, the use of musical ring tones on mobile phones was banned. In a later and more surreal development, the al-Shabaab militia in Jowhar in April 2010 banned the use of bells to mark the end of lessons in schools. It said the ringing sound too closely resembled that of Christian church bells; schoolteachers were ordered that from now on they should clap their hands at the end of each class.

In the same month, the Hizbul Islam movement ordered radio stations to stop playing music, threatening to kill those who disobeyed the new rule. The day after the ban was imposed, residents of Mogadishu woke up to recordings of gunfire coming from their radio sets instead of the usual music and jingles. Journalists at the radio stations decided to broadcast these sounds as a way of mocking the Islamists; with typical Somali humour, they also played sounds of croaking frogs. Ali Sheikh Yassin of the Mogadishu-based Elman Human Rights Organization, said: 'Here we are, talking about music as a sin against Islam, yet the biggest sin of all, killing humans, is being committed every hour of every day. The stations have come up with a very funny and novel way of dealing with this ban, but I am afraid the insurgents will come up with more draconian edicts.'[12]

There seems to be no limit to the ways al-Shabaab tries to control behaviour, progressively curbing people's freedoms. In January 2011, I was sitting in the lobby of a hotel in Hargeisa, the capital of Somaliland, when I was told about al-Shabaab's latest ruling, which banned men and women from shaking hands in public. It was early evening, and all around me in the hotel were Somali men and women, gathering to drink tea, talk politics and watch football on TV. Men dressed in colourful sarongs, flicking richly embroidered shawls over their shoulders, greeted the brightly dressed, bejewelled women by not only shaking their hands but lightly kissing them as is the traditional Somali way. I had arrived that day from Mogadishu, where the only women I saw were hidden away under thick dark robes; the contrast with the freedom and laughter of that Hargeisa hotel could not have been greater. The mood of the evening was light and romantic; men graciously quoted Somali poems to their female companions. Flirtation was subtle and refined, but it was in the atmosphere. I asked the Islamist leader Sheikh Hassan Dahir Aweys why he was so intent on imposing a form of Islam that crushed Somali customs:

I am shocked by the fact you could ask me such a question. First of all, the West needs to tell us why they are using their own draconian measures, such as mistreating the prisoners they have captured from al-Qaeda. Why are you concerned if we implement our Islamic law? It is a well-known fact that Islamic law is very helpful for society.

When it comes to the Islamic dress code, it is from God's law and it is in the Quran. Hijab is not forced on women but they chose to wear it to comply with God's law. What I find amazing is that Western countries want to force upon us their ways of going around naked. That is a very dangerous enterprise.

When it comes to the punishment of people by stoning them alive, first of all, this is a religious law and a religious commitment. If the Western countries refuse to apply God's law, it is their problem. But we are committed to implementing religious law. Practices such as stoning provide tangible benefits to society and to people in general.

At the same time as it was banning music from the radio, and ordering the closure of radio and television stations, al-Shabaab was introducing an ever more sophisticated propaganda machine of its own. In 2011 it launched its own television channel, al-Kataib, which was broadcast using the offices and equipment of the 'Voice of Peace', a TV station it had captured in Mogadishu.

Al-Kataib broadcasts footage of alleged spies making their confessions before they are executed; it plays interviews with al-Shabaab commanders and shows them making long speeches in front of large crowds. In stereotypical jihadi style, the commanders are often flanked by fighters in camouflage jackets, waving the black flag of al-Shabaab, their faces hidden by balaclavas or scarves. It shows mass religious gatherings, the streets packed as far as the eye can see with people praying, rhythmically kneeling and bowing their heads to the ground. A teenager in the bush undergoes military training, proudly holding up a paper target he has managed to riddle with bullet holes. Rousing jihadi songs are played; slick graphics with violent images fill the screen. Suddenly, there are shots of toddlers in a crowd, holding guns and pointing them at the camera.

Al-Shabaab has taken advantage of Somalis' love for the Internet by launching sophisticated websites; as soon as one site is closed down, another one opens. The web pages are filled with photos of dusty landscapes recently 'captured' by al-Shabaab, and gruesome images of dead civilians, their bodies smashed to pieces allegedly by AMISOM peacekeepers and government troops. There are photos of a Ugandan peacekeeper captured by al-Shabaab, his eyes darting back and forth in terror; at the time of writing he had still not been released after months in captivity.

Al-Shabaab also uses the Internet in order to raise money, holding live online fund-raising events, often for days at a time. A UN report describes a three-day fund-raiser in May 2009, and another two-week Internet event specifically to raise funds for al-Shabaab fighters in central Somalia:

> Al-Shabaab's Salahudiin Centre in Mogadishu directly
> coordinated and facilitated the event, which was attended
> by hundreds of participants in the diaspora … al-Shabaab
> regional leaders briefed the forum on the hardships facing
> the mujahideen and their families in those regions as victims
> of drought and conflict. The forum participants made pledges
> totalling over $40,000.[13]

With its advanced propaganda system available to anyone who has access to the Internet, al-Shabaab attracts supporters from all over the world, especially Somalis in the diaspora. But once people join the movement, whether voluntarily or by forced recruitment, it can, says the former al-Shabaab fighter Al Ahzari, be very difficult for them to leave:

> In 2010, I decided to leave al-Shabaab. My unit of fighters was

defeated on the battlefield. My superiors asked me personally to eliminate all my men who had been injured. It was then I realized al-Shabaab was against Somalis and their religion, so I defected.

I was only able to leave because I am protected by the government. Al-Shabaab usually slaughters people who defect because it is afraid they will spread its secrets. It is incredibly rare for someone to escape like I have. You can join al-Shabaab freely but it is almost impossible to leave.

Importing and exporting jihad

In contrast to the situation inside Somalia, where young men and boys have been forced to join al-Shabaab against their will, some Somalis living outside the country are desperate to join the group. Some have given up lives in Europe and the USA to blow themselves up as suicide bombers in Somalia. Since being labelled by the USA and others as a significant player in the global jihad and a key part of the al-Qaeda brand, al-Shabaab has attracted an increasing number of non-Somali foreign fighters, including South Asians, Arabs and Africans from other countries. The US Assistant Secretary of State, Jonnie Carson, spoke of the concerns about foreign fighters with possible al-Qaeda links fighting alongside al-Shabaab: 'We are extremely worried about the reports, and they do seem to be fairly serious and credible reports, that al-Shabaab does have amongst its fighters a number of individuals of South Asian and Chechnyan origin. This is a very disturbing situation and reflects the seriousness of the problem in Somalia.'

There appears, in particular, to be a 'special relationship' between jihadis from Somalia and Yemen. This is not surprising given the geographical proximity of the two countries and US attitudes towards them, the existence of a substantial Somali community in Yemen, and perhaps most importantly, the fact that the governments of both countries are weak or close to collapse. As the stability of Yemen continues to fracture, it is possible that the Islamist insurgencies in the two countries will become even more closely linked. A spokesman for al-Shabaab said in 2009 that both sides were providing each other with fighters.

Osama bin Laden, who was leader of al-Qaeda at the time, boosted Somalia's profile as a jihadi destination when in 2009 he released an eleven-minute audio message focusing entirely on the country. The message was entitled 'Fight on, champions of Somalia' and was dedicated 'To my patient, persevering Muslim brothers in Mujahid Somalia'. Osama bin Laden urged Somalis to overthrow the country's new president, Sheikh Sharif Sheikh Ahmed, a former leader of the Union of Islamic Courts, whom he accused of abandoning his religion to join the government, or as he put it to 'partner with the infidel'. He spoke of Somalia's Islamists as an important front in the global jihad, recognizing them as equal partners in the struggle: 'You are the first line of defence for the Islamic world in its south-western part; and your patience and resolve support your brothers in Palestine, Iraq, Afghanistan, the Islamic Maghreb, Pakistan and the rest of the fields of jihad.'

The killing of Osama bin Laden by US special forces in May 2011 received mixed reactions in Somalia. Women celebrated on the streets of government-held parts of Mogadishu, rejoicing in the death of the man they said was ultimately responsible for the killing of their loved ones. Al-Shabaab issued a statement saying it would avenge his death; some of its fighters wore white as a sign of grief.

It is impossible to know exactly how many foreign fighters have joined the jihad in Somalia, and which countries they come from, but they have a significant presence. The former al-Shabaab fighter Al Ahzar described how foreign jihadis in Somalia operate as separate units within the insurgency:

I fought alongside several units of foreign fighters. There are about 1,800 foreign jihadis in Somalia. They are in some ways the leadership of al-Shabaab. They fight in special units of their own and their main base is in Mogadishu. They include Arabs, Pakistanis, white people – even Americans – and many Africans including Kenyans, Sudanese, Ethiopians and Eritreans.

Many of these foreigners are criminals in their own countries. A Bangladeshi fighter told me he had been in prison for fifteen years, but had escaped and come to Somalia. He said he did not want law and order to return to Somalia because it is so easy to hide here when there is chaos. The foreigners want Somalia to remain stateless because this is what makes it such a good refuge for them.

Many Somalis from the diaspora come and work with the foreign units as drivers, translators and foot soldiers. They come to Somalia to martyr themselves. Those Somalis who are not in any trouble in the diaspora, who are not under suspicion, are often sent back there for foreign operations. They are prepared to wait years to carry out attacks overseas. They don't care how long it takes. There are sleeping cells of jihadis in places like Holland, the USA and Britain, working on projects to attack those countries.

The Islamist leader Hassan Dahir Aweys also spoke about foreign fighters:

What is wrong with getting help from other people if your enemy is more powerful than you, and has more weapons? What is wrong if we get some help? If people, who are poor and weak, organize themselves to fight against their enemy, what is wrong with them getting help from any quarter they can get it from?

Most of the foreign fighters in al-Shabaab are ethnic Somalis living in the diaspora and in possession of US or European citizenship. They started to leave for Somalia after the Ethiopian invasion of December 2006; the CIA said the invasion 'catalyzed' expatriate Somalis to join the Islamist extremists. Given that Ethiopia's action had US backing, it would be more accurate to say it was the joint US–Ethiopian action which radicalized Somalis in the diaspora, pushing them to fight jihad in their homeland. One of the returnee jihadis was Shirwa Ahmed, a twenty-six-year-old Somali US citizen from Minnesota, who dropped out of college to go and fight for al-Shabaab. He blew himself up in October 2008, driving a car packed with explosives into a government building in Puntland, north-eastern Somalia. He has been described by the US media as 'the first known American suicide bomber'.[14]

Shirwa Ahmed was one of several young Somali men from Minnesota's largest city, Minneapolis, to join al-Shabaab. The FBI estimates that, between September 2007 and October 2009, more than twenty Somalis left Minnesota to join the Islamist insurgency in Somalia. Minneapolis is the capital of Somalia's diaspora in the USA; one run-down part of the city is known as 'Mini Mogadishu', the same name Kenyans have given the district of Eastleigh in Nairobi. The US authorities are so concerned about Somali extremism that the FBI has set up a Joint Terrorism Task Force in Minneapolis:

> Since late 2006, we have seen several individuals from the United States – many with ethnic ties to Somalia and some without such connections – travel to Somalia to train or fight on behalf of al-Shabaab. The number of individuals we believe have departed for Somalia is comparatively larger than the number of individuals who have left the United States for other conflict zones around the world over the past few years. And we have seen more individuals leave from the Minneapolis area than from any other part of the country.[15]

The greatest fear is that US-based Somalis will one day carry out what the FBI has described as 'terrorist activity' on American soil. In February 2010, the American Director of National Intelligence, Dennis Blair, told a Senate Select Committee hearing on 'Current and Projected Threats to the United States' that he believed some of those training and fighting in Somalia could redirect their activities to the USA.

The USA has taken action against American Somalis; in August 2010, fourteen people were charged with acts of terrorism, including providing money, personnel and other material support to al-Shabaab. Two were arrested, the remaining twelve were believed to have already left for Somalia. According to the US Attorney General Eric Holder, 'these indictments and arrests shed further light on a deadly pipeline that has routed funding and fighters to al-Shabaab from cities across the US'.

In July 2011, a twenty-six-year-old Somali from Minneapolis, Omer Abdi Mohamed, pleaded guilty in a federal court to conspiring to provide material support to a conspiracy to murder, kidnap and maim abroad. According to the US Attorney, B. Todd Jones:

> Those involved in this conspiracy, including Omer Abdi
> Mohamed, violated the law in a dangerous and misguided
> effort to support a terrorist organization. In the process, they
> tore apart many Somali-American families. Parents were left
> to fret over the disappearance of their young sons, who often
> left home without a word. In some instances family members
> discovered what happened to their relatives only by watching
> internet videos being used as propaganda by al-Shabaab.[16]

The FBI 'Operation Rhino' investigation, which focused on young Somali men from Minneapolis, found that they had for several years been returning home to fight:

> The earliest groups of identified travelers departed the

United States in October and December 2007, while others left in February 2008, August 2008, November 2008 and October 2009. Upon arriving in Somalia, the men resided in al-Shabaab safe-houses in southern Somalia until constructing an al-Shabaab training camp where they were trained. Senior members of al-Shabaab and a senior member of al-Qaeda in East Africa conducted the training.[17]

Some of the US Somalis who have joined al-Shabaab are marginalized members of the community, belonging to gangs such as the 'Rough Tough Somalis' and 'Murda Squad'. Jihad is, in a sense, another form of teenage rebellion, the modern-day rock and roll. Information about Somali Islamist extremism is readily available on the Internet; there are plenty of websites and chat-rooms linked to al-Shabaab, and, to a disaffected Somali living in Minnesota, they offer excitement, glamour and a purpose. As a jihadi posted on one al-Shabaab website, 'There is no way to understand the sweetness of jihad until you come to jihad.' The Internet enables those who have already left for Somalia to encourage others to join them, 'bigging up' the thrill and importance of what they are doing. One Facebook message posted by a Somali who had recently left the USA for Mogadishu said, 'Sup dawg, bring yourself over here to M-town ... where men carry all types of guns.'[18] Other diaspora fighters are more educated, dropping out of college courses to go and wage war in Somalia.

Young Somalis with European citizenship are also leaving to join al-Shabaab. In the UK, which is home to the largest Somali community in Europe, the security services estimate dozens have left. One was a twenty-one-year-old man from Ealing, West London, who, in October 2007, blew himself up at a checkpoint in the southern Somali town of Baidoa, killing about twenty government soldiers. According to the Somali authorities, the 2009 suicide bombing of a graduation ceremony in Mogadishu was carried out by a Somali from Denmark who had dressed himself up as a woman. It is not clear why so many of the suicide bombers in Somalia have been young men from the diaspora rather than local recruits.

Of greatest concern to foreign governments is the fear, and growing reality, of Somalis perpetrating attacks outside Somalia. Although the main direction of travel has been the return to Somalia by members of the diaspora, attacks have been perpetrated by Somali Islamists outside the country. The most deadly was the killing of more than seventy people in Uganda by al-Shabaab suicide bombers. There are other examples, from farther afield than Africa. The Australian security services announced in August 2009 that they had uncovered a plot by immigrants, including three Somalis with Australian citizenship, to carry out a suicide attack on an army base in Sydney. Three of the four men convicted of the botched bombing on the London Underground on 21 July 2005 were Somalis. The former British minister for Africa, Lord Malloch Brown, said in 2009 that Somalia represented a greater threat to the UK than Afghanistan.

The image of Somalia as a major African front in the 'War on Terror', and the export of violence from the country, means that Somalis have a 'bad name' in many countries, and are sometimes wrongly accused of violent Islamist activity. In 2009, I spoke to the Somali Mohamed Suleiman Barre, shortly after he was released from prison in Guantánamo. He had been locked up there for several years before being released and sent home to the self-declared republic of Somaliland:

> I was arrested in Pakistan in 2001 and accused of terrorist activities. Pakistani intelligence officials took me to a jail where they hold terrorist suspects. I was kept there for nearly four months. American personnel visited me three times for questioning. They said they had traced my phone calls and

that I had been contacted by high-level terrorist suspects. They forced me to admit things I had not done.

Then three other people and I were transferred to Bagram airbase in Afghanistan where we were tortured very badly. They did terrible things to us. They later sent me to Guantánamo Bay where I spent many years, most of them in solitary confinement. My mind became completely broken.

I feel like someone who has just emerged from a grave. It will take me some time to adapt to the real world. All I want to do is to live as a normal person. I still don't know why they arrested me in the first place. After being held for eight years, they released me without charge.

It is possible that the increased monitoring and targeting of Somalis around the world will, like the Ethiopian invasion of 2006, further radicalize the Somali community, leading to more attacks at home and abroad.

It would be wrong to argue that, prior to the rise of the UIC, there was no violent Islamism in Somalia; as this chapter has shown, extremist groups had existed for years, although always on the margins. The 2011 killing in Mogadishu of the head of al-Qaeda in East Africa, Fazul Abdullah Mohamed, proves that Somalia has served as a haven for senior international al-Qaeda operatives. It is unclear whether Fazul Abdullah Mohamed made Somalia his base before or after the rise of al-Shabaab, but the fact that by the late 2000s the movement controlled much of south-central Somalia, including large parts of the capital city, made the country a more attractive option as a safe haven for senior international Islamist figures.

Once again, the USA and its allies misjudged events in Somalia. They assumed too quickly that the Union of Islamic Courts constituted a threat. This misperception may well have inadvertently contributed to the rise of violent Islamism in the country. It might have been more productive if foreign powers had recognized and built upon the positive achievements of the UIC, engaging with it and supporting its state-building initiatives. Instead, they drove it from power, destroying what was the most successful attempt since 1991 to restore order in south-central Somalia. The end result of this policy was the emergence of the far more radical al-Shabaab movement, which has taken on an international dimension, attracting foreign fighters and giving rise to the fear that Somalis will carry out violent Islamist attacks on American soil.

4 | A FAILED STATE?

I am standing in the 'Somalia' section of the library in the School of Oriental and African Studies in London. As I cast my eye along the shelves, these are the sort of titles that leap out at me: *Somalia: A Government at War with Its Own People*, *The Fallen State*, *From Bad Policy to Chaos in Somalia*, *Somalia Undone*, *Hostages: The People Who Kidnapped Themselves*, *The Betrayal of the Somalis*, *The Road to Zero: Somalia's Self Destruction* ... There is an overwhelming sense of ruin, failure and hopelessness.

The dominant image of Somalia is of a stateless, 'failed' country whose inhabitants have lost control of their destinies; a place where everything has collapsed, where violence and hunger dominate. The aim of this chapter is to challenge the conventional view of Somalia, to tell another story. Hardship and danger cannot be ignored but they should not be allowed to totally eclipse the positive developments in the territory since 1991.

Somalia regularly comes top of lists of the world's failed states, scoring high on every social, economic and political indicator of 'failure'.[1] In the 2010 'Failed State Index' compiled by the US think tank the Fund for Peace, Somalia, like an Olympic champion, scored a 'perfect 10' for three of the twelve indicators, and high '9s' for most of the others. In 2011, for the fourth year running, it came top of the list again.

Media reports and some lengthier, more thorough studies by human rights groups, think tanks, academics and others frequently refer to Somalia as a 'failed state', leading to the impression that nothing works in the country, that it is a bloodbath, awash with disorder. Such an image is misleading, and has in all likelihood contributed to misguided attitudes and policies, not just on the part of foreign governments, but also aid organizations, pressure groups, potential investors and others.

Dealing with perceived 'failed states' has become a key part of US foreign policy. The 2002 US National Security Strategy stated that 'America is now threatened less by conquering states than we are by failing ones'. The 2008 US National Defense Strategy also regarded state 'failure' as a potentially serious security threat: 'The inability of many states to police themselves effectively or to work with their neighbours to ensure regional security represents a challenge to the international system ... If left unchecked, such instability can spread and threaten regions of interest to the United States, our allies, and friends.'

The term 'failed state' is not a neutral definition. Noam Chomsky has devoted a whole book applying the term to the United States.[2] Some descriptions of what constitutes a 'failed state' are useful when discussing Somalia, but they should not be applied as blanket terms; they should only be used to describe certain parts of the country at certain periods in its history. The Crisis States Research Centre at the London School of Economics describes a 'failed state' as one 'that can no longer perform its basic security and development functions and that has no effective control over its territory and borders'. This is of relevance to parts of Somalia, particularly the southern and central regions. Also helpful is the American academic Robert Rotberg's definition of a 'failed state' as a territory that is 'tense, deeply conflicted, dangerous and bitterly contested by warring factions' and 'hospitable to and harbouring non-state actors – warlords and terrorists'.[3]

Although, to all intents and purposes, the central state has 'failed' in Somalia, it would be wrong to assume that the failure of government has led to the inevitable collapse of everything else in the country. One reason why media and other reports frequently give the impression that the whole of Somalia has 'failed' is because the situation is often portrayed through a lens too tightly focused on the capital, Mogadishu, where civilians are killed on an almost daily basis in chaotic, unpredictable violence involving al-Qaeda-linked fighters, clan militias, bandits, forces loyal to an ineffective 'central government' and peacekeeping troops from the African Union. The addition of pirates, foreign hostages and attacks by Somali Islamists on other countries has created a 'perfect storm' for the media. Somalia contains a rich set of ingredients for a 'bad news story', and is therefore an excellent source of media fodder, closely conforming to prevailing stereotypes of Africa. As Ian Birrell of the *Observer* newspaper has put it:

> Think of Africa and for too many people it conjures up images of hunger, poverty, disease and conflict. These are the four horsemen of the supposed African apocalypse. Journalists seeking stories look for death, decay and destruction while charities seeking donations reinforce the stereotypes with pictures of malnourished children and dying adults.[4]

Because these 'four horsemen', and several others besides, exist in Somalia, it is easy for journalists to sell it to their editors as the ultimate 'African apocalypse' story. Audiences are especially receptive to apocalyptic accounts of Africa because that is what they have been primed to expect. The situation in Somalia can be fitted so neatly into the narrative of 'death, decay and destruction' that media stories about the country almost write themselves, even though they often end up presenting a limited and distorted picture of the reality on the ground.

I confess that when I write news stories about violence in Mogadishu, I tend to slip into autopilot, my fingers rapidly tapping out the familiar lines. I often find myself starting with the sentence, 'Medical staff in the Somali capital, Mogadishu, say at least *x* people have been killed in fighting between Islamist insurgents and government troops backed by peacekeepers from the African Union.' I use the phrase 'at least' before stating the number of people who have been killed, because the figure usually rises as the day goes on.

As descriptions of Somalia are so often locked into narrow stereotypes, many people have not been given the opportunity of understanding the country as anything other than a 'failed' or 'rogue' state, of immense danger to itself and increasingly to the wider world. The 'failed state' label has proved convenient for some actors, including the United States, who have used it to justify their policies towards Somalia. Presenting the situation in such a restricted way not only prevents people from seeing the true picture on the ground; it has also led to misguided policies that have backfired not only within Somalia but sometimes on the outside powers trying to implement them.

Somalia does not fit into any familiar paradigm of 'statehood' but this does not mean that it is in a state of total disintegration. Even in Mogadishu, which has been affected by almost continual violence for the past twenty years, there is some kind of order; many things are still 'working'. For example, there is a functioning ambulance service, with staff risking their lives on an almost daily basis to drive around the city, retrieving the dead and injured.

When I arrived at Mogadishu airport in January 2011, it was freshly painted and orderly; burly white men with crew cuts and tight T-shirts, working for a company called SKA, directed operations with military efficiency. On the plane from Nairobi to Mogadishu were Somali businesspeople and large family groups returning home from their holidays. I sat next to a glamorous Somali woman who lived in Canada but was coming to explore financial opportunities in Mogadishu. 'There is a lot of money to be made here,' she told me. 'I plan to make lucrative deals providing supplies to the African Union peacekeepers.'

Mini-states

One part of Somalia where the term 'failed state' most definitely does not apply is the self-declared republic of Somaliland,
where the territory is rebuilding itself from the rubble of war into
a functioning state. Although it is not recognized internationally,
Somaliland has a growing economy and a democratic political
system that works better than many others on the continent. As
will be discussed later in this chapter, it has been experiencing quite the opposite of state 'failure' since it declared itself
independent in 1991.

Somaliland is the most impressive example of progress and
stability, but other parts of Somali territory are also functioning
as viable political units, with varying degrees of success. Bordering
Somaliland is the semi-autonomous region of Puntland, which
since 1998 has had its own president, government and regional
administration. It has not followed the example of Somaliland
by declaring itself independent; instead it operates as a sort of
'mini-state' within Somalia. Puntland has encountered several
difficulties; it is involved in a long-running and at times violent
border dispute with Somaliland, it has experienced a number of
political upheavals, some of them violent, and, for some years,
it served as a major base for piracy. But conditions in this large
stretch of territory should not be equated with the far more
volatile and violent situation farther south.

The declaration of semi-autonomous 'mini-states' has become
fashionable in recent years, particularly among Somali politicians
from the diaspora. In 2011, some of these 'statelets' were operating as semi-viable units, including the central Somali regions
of Himan and Heeb, which had a 'president' from the Somali
diaspora in the United States, and Galmudug, whose 'president'
was a British Somali. They were, however, extremely weak, and
vulnerable to attack by al-Shabaab and other armed groups.
The populations of these regions appeared to view the local

administrations as more legitimate and effective than the central government in Mogadishu. When, for example, in November 2010, the British couple Paul and Rachel Chandler were released by Somali pirates after more than a year in captivity, the 'authority' to whom they were handed over was the 'president' of the Adaado region, Mohamed Adan. It was Mr Adan who alerted me by telephone to the Chandlers' imminent release, and when, where and how it would happen. He later called to tell me the couple had been safely handed over to him, that they had been given what he described as 'a refreshing shower' and 'a delicious breakfast'. The Chandlers were later flown to Mogadishu to have their photographs taken with members of the transitional administration in what was little more than a media stunt to give the impression to the watching world that the central government had been in charge of the release operation.

Some of Somalia's 'mini-states' must not be taken too seriously as they exist in little more than name. They are essentially mirages, part of the fantasy land of exiled politicians who crave power but have very little. The creation of one such territory was announced in March 2011 by the former defence minister, Mohamed Abdi, better known as 'Professor Gandhi'. He declared the formation of the new region of 'Azania', a large stretch of southern Somalia extending from the strategic southern port of Kismayo to the Kenyan border. The fact that 'Professor Gandhi' made his declaration from Kenya, and that much of 'Azania', including its capital Kismayo, was under the control of al-Shabaab, meant his announcement was virtually meaningless.

Although it was the collapse of central government which allowed al-Shabaab and other Islamist groups to emerge as powerful forms of alternative authority, the areas they control cannot be described as anarchic or lawless. The large parts of southern and central Somalia controlled by Islamist militias function according to strict rules; a form of 'extreme order' has been imposed.

The traditional Somali way of life has been severely restricted and many freedoms lost, but areas under the firm control of al-Shabaab are often safer than many other parts of the country. Several friends and colleagues who work in violent and unstable parts of Somalia, especially Mogadishu, have sent their families to live in al-Shabaab-occupied areas because they are far safer, as long as people keep to the rules.

The experience of Somalia since the fall of Siad Barre offers fascinating examples of how society works without an effective central government, and demonstrates the inventiveness and resilience of the Somalis. Somaliland is the most mature and stable of the new political formations, followed by Puntland. Territories controlled by al-Shabaab offer an Islamist alternative. There are several other examples of more localized forms of order, although they are often unstable and confined to small areas. They include power bases run by warlords, clan leaders, business cartels and religious groups. As will be discussed in the next chapter, mini-societies and mini-economies have even developed in regions controlled by pirates.

The economy

One of the most interesting success stories during the period of 'state failure' in Somalia is the economy, which has shown extraordinary resilience, adapting to and sometimes taking advantage of the lack of strong central government. Peter Little has written a fascinating book, *Somalia: Economy without State*, which describes how some sectors of the economy, particularly livestock, have flourished in the absence of central authority; he presents a very different picture of the country from that so often portrayed in the media and other reports:

Since the collapse of any vestiges of central government in
1991, it has been difficult to match the descriptions of chaos,

hunger and anarchy that frequently appear in the Western media with my own accounts of Somali social and economic life. There is a glaring disconnect ... Depending on one's perspective, Somalia can invoke both elements of economic optimism – a freewheeling, stateless capitalism – and political pessimism. On the global landscape it embodies the 'never never' land of non-states and failed diplomacy and represents the longest period of any nation in modern history without a government.[5]

Other studies, based on statistics from the United Nations, the World Bank and other international institutions, also show how, contrary to expectations, the economy of Somalia has actually grown during the many years without effective central authority. A report by the US-based Independent Institute explains how

Far from chaos and economic collapse, we find that Somalia is generally doing better than when it had a state. Basic economic order is possible because of the existence of a common law dispute resolution system and a non-state monetary system. On that foundation we find that urban business and commercial activity is possible and that the pastoral sector has expanded ... Urban businessmen, international corporations, and rural pastoralists have all functioned in stateless Somalia, achieving standards of living for the country that are equal or superior to many other African nations.[6]

The Independent Institute examined thirteen indicators, including death rate and life expectancy, and found that, although living standards in Somalia were low by Western standards, they compared fairly favourably with those in other countries in Africa.[7] Somalia ranked in the top 50 per cent of African countries on six of the thirteen indicators, and near the bottom on only three – infant mortality, access to improved water resources, and immunization rates. Some indicators, such as telecommunications, have improved dramatically since the fall of central authority, with Somalia moving from twenty-ninth to eighth position in the list of African countries.

In a study for West Virginia University, Peter Leeson looks at how eighteen development indicators have changed since the collapse of effective central government.[8] Comparing data from 1985–90 with those from 2000–05, he found that Somalia was doing better without a central state than when it had one. Scores for thirteen of the eighteen indicators had clearly improved since the collapse of the state, and had declined for only two: adult literacy and school enrolment.

Care must be taken with analyses based on statistics from Somalia. It has been all but impossible to gather reliable data from within the country since the late 1980s owing to the dangerous situation on the ground and the fact that many ministries and other government departments have been destroyed, and with them all of their documents.

These studies present a surprisingly positive picture of Somalia, but they cannot disguise the fact that hundreds of thousands of Somalis live on the very edge of existence. Most of the civilians left in Mogadishu are those who cannot afford to leave. According to the United Nations, the more than 400,000 people living in largely temporary shelters along the road from Mogadishu to the town of Afgoye had by 2010 become the largest concentration of internally displaced people in the world. The area, known as the 'Afgoye Corridor', has become the third-largest urban concentration in Somalia, after Mogadishu and Hargeisa. Satellite images show how what was a fairly sparsely populated area in 2007 became a city of the displaced just three years later.[9] The UN estimates that more than 20 per cent of Somalia's population of approximately ten million is either internally displaced or living abroad as refugees. While dynamic entrepreneurs have made huge profits from state collapse, millions of others are completely desperate.

In January 2011, I met a woman, Uwah, who had recently fled from Mogadishu to Nairobi. She was standing on the side of a potholed road, lorries and minibuses roaring past her. In front of her was a small rickety table, with a few second-hand baby clothes arranged neatly on top. She was dressed entirely in black, including her gloves and socks; the only thing I could see was the flash of her eyes:

> I left Mogadishu because of the shells, the rockets and the bullets. I left because of the war going on day after endless day. I left because I couldn't make any money to feed my children. My husband was killed in the fighting so I have nobody else to rely on.
>
> I left my children in Mogadishu because I couldn't afford to bring them here. I feel sick with worry about them but how could I help them when I was there? I could not make a living because of all the fighting. I paid two hundred US dollars to come here. I travelled by lorry from Mogadishu to the Kenyan border, then took another vehicle down to Nairobi. I pray that I will make some money here so that I can send it back home to my little ones.

The lack of effective central government brings with it certain economic freedoms and opportunities, but businesspeople are, like everybody else in Somalia, restricted by violence and insecurity. They still have to pay taxes and fees to faction leaders, local administrations, Islamist groups, port militias and armed men at roadblocks but, as Little writes, 'levels of taxation and trade restrictions are considerably lower than they were pre-1991'.[10]

Somali society is probably better suited than most others to coping without central authority; it is possible that many other parts of the world would have experienced a far deeper and more widespread form of collapse if they had lived for so many years without government. The threat of violence and almost constant movement have long been key elements of Somalia's nomadic culture. Traditional systems such as the *diya* blood compensation scheme offer a form of insurance, *xeer* offers a form of law, and money and other goods can be exchanged on a trust basis through clan-based networks. As Anna Lindley has written:

> One positive side of 'statelessness' is that Somalia has benefit-ted from the absence of restrictive and over-bureaucratic business laws and other regulations that are so prevalent in other parts of Africa, stifling the spirit of entrepreneurship and inhibiting growth ... Many commentators have noted that the Somali civil war ironically resembled, in its outcomes, a radical structural adjustment programme: it entirely freed the economy from state regulation – liberalising foreign trade, free-ing exchange rates, eliminating subsidies, destroying the public sector, and privatising parastatals.[11]

Somalis' nomadic culture has given them a head start for conducting business in the twenty-first century. They are already mobile and globalized. They are used to being on the move with their possessions, communicating with people in different parts of the world, and moving money and goods around with little regard for national borders. Many also have a certain chutzpah, in the positive sense of the word, whereby they dare to do and ask for things most others would not. I sat with a Somali businessman in a London restaurant as he hammered out multiple deals on his various mobile phones, sent endless emails from his iPad, devoured a large plate of spaghetti bolognaise, asked me to write an email to a client on his BlackBerry, and summoned over the waiter brandishing a pile of paper. 'Just fax these documents to this number for me,' he demanded, with a cheeky smile and so much confidence that the waiter simply nodded and ran off to complete the task. The businessman does not let his location get in the way of what he is doing. He operates from Mogadishu, Dubai, London and Nairobi. He is as at home sitting under a tree in Somalia chewing *qat* with his camel-herder cousins as he is in a London boardroom. He is a postmodern nomad with a very healthy bank account.

Another reason for their relative economic success is the risk-taking, entrepreneurial nature of many Somali businesspeople. I asked the Nairobi-based Somali businessman Sheikh Shakul to tell me the secret of Somali success in business:

> I think you need to be a Somali to understand this! One thing that is unique about Somalis is the issue of trust. People will come to you, they will give you their money without signing any document, they will say, 'Here is my money, help me', and five or six people will come together entirely due to trust. This is one of the main assets we have. If someone wants to open a shop somewhere, he will call his cousins in London, South Africa, Mogadishu or Mombasa, and they will contribute. They will enable him to open the shop, and he will do the same thing for others. Trust is the secret of the success of the Somalis. Also, Somalis are amazingly energetic and dynamic. Because of the war in Somalia, there is no central government, there are no institutions to help people, so everybody has do their own thing, you have to depend on yourself. Everybody has relatives who are suffering, so everyone feels responsible for doing things for other people. The war is one of the main reasons behind all this energy and entrepreneurial activity.

Despite the absence of a functioning government, economic agreements have been forged with neighbouring countries and transnational businesses. On a flight I took to Mogadishu during the height of the civil war in the early 1990s, the only other people on the plane were two Filipino businessmen from the multinational Dole Fruit company. They were coming to discuss possible trade deals with faction leaders who controlled the banana plantations and other fruit-growing areas. Peter Little offers other examples of the international business presence in Somalia:

> The lack of a recognised government and of national institutions, such as a treasury or judicial system, does not discourage legitimate international firms from dealing with Somalia, including its breakaway states in the north. Dole Fruit Inc had investments in Somalia's agricultural sector in the 1990s, as did Italian agribusiness companies. Somalia currently is served by international couriers, such as DHL, and by automobile companies, such as General Motors of Kenya.[12]

Livestock

The trade in livestock, Somalia's most valuable commodity, has flourished since the collapse of the state. This is partly because the nomads who look after the goats, sheep, cows and camels have a lifestyle that never had much to do with central authority. Their way of life is in many ways incompatible with a formal, centralized state; they tend to ignore national borders and have their own traditional social structures and legal and economic systems. The nomads in some ways gained more than they lost with the collapse of Siad Barre's administration, which had become increasingly predatory and obstructive. It is possible that the traditional nomadic way of life has been strengthened by the lack of organized government; people have been able to revert to their simpler, older way of doing things.

It is, however, remarkable that despite so many years of conflict and disruption, Somalia's pastoral economy has, according to Little, remained a regional leader, stronger than its more stable neighbours of Ethiopia and Kenya: 'Somalia (including Somaliland) remains a major player in livestock trade on a regional and global scale, accounting for more than 60 per cent of all livestock exports from East Africa during the 1990s.'[13]

Little says the flow of livestock from Somalia to Kenya and other foreign markets has increased dramatically since the fall of Siad Barre. In a chapter aptly entitled 'Boom times in a bust state', he describes 'the spectacular surge' in cross-border livestock trade with Kenya, focusing on sales in the Kenyan town of Garissa, near the border with Somalia: 'The aggregate value of cattle sales in Garissa grew by an astounding 400 per cent between 1991 and 1998 and 600 per cent between 1989 and 1998. In terms of volume, annual sales grew from 24,395 in 1989 to more than 100,000 cattle in 1998.'[14]

The figures for trade to the Gulf states are equally dramatic:

The overseas trade in small stock (goats and sheep) from Somaliland and neighbouring Puntland was larger in volume in 1999 than before the government's collapse. In the 1980s Somalia was one of the largest exporters of live animals in the world ... In 1999 the northern ports of Bossaso and Berbera exported about 2.9 million head of small stock. Moreover, the two Somali ports accounted for 95 per cent of all goat and 52 per cent of sheep exports for the entire eastern Africa region, an amazing achievement for a 'stateless' society.[15]

Despite the boom, the livestock trade is precarious. Nomads are not immune from the violence that has at times forced them to change the routes they have followed for centuries. Young male nomads, with their strength, high endurance levels and knowledge of the terrain, are a particularly attractive target for recruitment by al-Shabaab and other armed groups. Some have been forcibly recruited into the militias, others join of their own will, attracted by the offer of money, spiritual gain or other benefits.

Communities dependent on the sale of their animals have been devastated by periodic bans imposed by the Saudi government on the import of livestock from Somali territories to prevent the spread of Rift Valley Fever. The region is also subject to frequent dry periods and drought, leading to the deaths of tens of thousands of heads of livestock, and the destruction of people's livelihoods. Some parts of Somalia were in 2011 affected by what the UN has described as the worst drought in sixty years, leading people to walk, sometimes for weeks, through hundreds of miles of conflict-ridden territory to reach already crowded refugee camps in Kenya and Ethiopia. Others left the countryside for Mogadishu, which, although racked by almost daily violence, seemed to them a better option than the parched land they came from.

Money transfer and telecommunications

Another remarkable success story has been the rapid expansion since the early 1990s of the money transfer and telecommunications sectors. This can in part be explained by the lack of state regulation and the need for a people scattered so far across the globe to stay in touch with and support each other.

After the collapse of effective central government, Somalis became increasingly reliant on their traditional ways of dealing with money, known as *hawala* or *xawilaad*. Unlike the livestock trade, which has not changed significantly for decades, except perhaps for the addition of the mobile phone as an essential part of the nomad's kit as it allows them to remotely check livestock prices, money transfer has become an ultra-modern globalized system. Somali money transfer systems are arguably the most advanced on the continent, using the latest technology to send funds all over the world.

The fusion of the traditional with the modern has worked especially well in this sector. The clan system guards against deception in business dealings, it allows defaulters to be tracked down with relative ease, and means informal background checks can be performed on potential business partners or agents. Somali customary law or *xeer* can be used to underwrite contracts and resolve financial disputes. Anna Lindley has written extensively on Somali remittances:

> Far from being just an intriguing financial mechanism used by a small number of migrants, *xawilaad* is a phenomenon of considerable scale and significance. In the absence of a banking system, it is this infrastructure that articulates the economic relationships between the Somali regions and the rest of the world – mediating remittances, trade, investment, aid, and political finance.[16]

The United Nations estimates that more than US$1.5 billion worth of remittances are sent to Somalia and Somaliland every year. At the time of writing, a significant amount of this was sent via the Dahabshiil money transfer company. It is ironic that Dahabshiil, one of the biggest money transfer businesses in Africa, is based in Somaliland, a breakaway territory whose independent status has not been recognized by anybody. It is a truly global business, operating in 150 countries, employing more than two thousand staff, with up to twenty thousand money transfer agents, some operating from offices in London, Sydney, Minneapolis and Toronto, others from kiosks in remote parts of Somalia, Ethiopia and South Sudan.

Dahabshiil started from humble beginnings in the north-western Somali town of Burao, where in 1970 Mohamed Said Duale opened a shop selling goods imported from Yemen and other parts of the world. As he needed Yemeni currency to buy his merchandise, he struck a deal with Somalis living in Aden whereby they would give him local currency to buy his goods; in exchange, he paid their relatives in Burao the equivalent amount in Somali currency. In this way, a small, informal money transfer system was born.

Mohamed Said Duale lost everything during the civil war in the

1980s, and was forced to flee Burao on foot with his family into the bush, and later to the refugee camps of Ethiopia. It was here that he saw a potentially lucrative business opportunity; Somalis living abroad wanted to send money to their relatives in the camps, so he restarted his business in a different form. The son of Dahabshiil's founder and CEO of the company, Abdirashid Duale, told me how the conflict led to extraordinary business growth:

> Even though we lost everything in the civil war, the international part of our money transfer business took off as a result of the conflict. Somali refugees were scattered all over the world, in Europe, the US, Australia and Asia. They were asking us, 'Why don't you open an office in Sweden, in Canada, there are a lot of Somalis here?', so we ended up expanding all over the world.[17]

Dahabshiil soon attracted the attention of aid agencies and other organizations, which saw it as a quick, reliable and inexpensive way of sending money to difficult and remote places in the Horn of Africa. In Dahabshiil's main office in Nairobi, I saw United Nations staff sending substantial amounts of money to their operations in Somalia. The company serves other communities in the region, including Rwandans and South Sudanese, who have also been affected by war and displaced far and wide.

Dahabshiil's multi-storey operational headquarters is in the centre of Hargeisa, surrounded by the chaos of informal trade. Women sell fresh green bunches of *qat* from small trolleys and kiosks, others serve sweet tea to men who spend hours talking politics in tiny 'cafés', sitting on rusty chairs in the dust, under shade provided by a few sheets of corrugated iron. Directly outside the building are the 'pavement banks'; men sit beside wire cages stacked high with Somali shillings, US dollars and other currencies. When they want to have lunch, they simply put the money inside the cage, lock the door and leave.

6 'Pavement banker' in Hargeisa (Mary Harper)

It is an altogether different world inside the Dahabshiil building. In the main computer room, giant machines whir and spin, lights flashing on and off, as money is electronically transferred across the world. On another floor, the room is split up into different geographical regions. The man on the 'South Asia desk' was busy sending a text message to someone in a remote village in Somaliland informing him that he could go to his local agent to collect the US$200 he had been sent by a relative in Bangladesh. Money is transferred in a matter of minutes; the company operates twenty-four hours a day, seven days a week, 365 days a year.

In another office, I was approached by a man smartly dressed in a dark suit, white shirt and a green Dahabshiil tie. 'Have you ever seen a million dollars in cash?' he asked. He then leaned down and opened a safe, throwing bundle after bundle of brand-new, tightly bound US$100 notes at me. Each bundle contained a thousand notes, or US$100,000, and many more than ten bundles came out of the safe. The array of currency was extraordinary, reflecting the truly globalized nature of the Somalis. Apart from the US dollars and Somaliland shillings, there were euros, Australian dollars, English pounds, Dubai dirhams, Kenyan shillings, Yemeni riyals and many more.

On the ground floor were long queues of businessmen, women in colourful robes, wild-haired nomads in sandals and simple tunics, and Somalilanders who had come on holiday to Hargeisa from the United States and other countries; all had come to send or receive money. One man had just received US$140 from a relative in Southall, London, a woman was sending money to a friend in Puntland, and another man was depositing some of his own money into an account he held at Dahabshiil.

Some Somali remittance companies have been accused of fuelling conflict by serving as conduits for the transfer of money to violent groups such as al-Shabaab. Shortly after the 9/11 attacks on the United States, the American authorities closed down what was at the time one of Somalia's biggest money transfer companies, al-Barakat, accusing it of channelling funds to al-Qaeda. This had a devastating effect on the Somalis dependent on it for remittances from overseas, as the funds they relied on for their survival were cut off.

Abdirashid Duale of Dahabshiil insists his company adheres to strict anti-money-laundering practices, and runs instant checks on its clients to make sure they are not on international lists of suspected criminals or members of banned groups:

> We make sure we are dealing with the right people; we identify
> them either in the Somali way through the clan system and
> by checking their IDs. We have to comply with international
> regulations. We and our agents are authorized by international
> regulators including the US Treasury Department, the British

Financial Services Authority, the Dubai Central Bank and several African financial institutions.

The highly developed nature of the large money transfer companies in Somalia has, according to Lindley, led to the development of other sectors of the economy: 'The sector rapidly incorporated new technologies to relay payment information, from radios to fax, mobile and satellite phones, to email and dedicated company software. Money transmitters' substantial investments helped drive Somalia's telecommunications revolution.'[18]

Somalia has taken a great leap into the future with telecommunications, leaving behind many more politically stable and economically developed countries in Africa. Like the Democratic Republic of the Congo, which also had limited central authority during the 1990s, Somalia was quick to adopt the mobile phone, with many people bypassing the landline phase altogether. It is no coincidence that Somalia's 'telecommunications revolution' happened at the same time as the state was collapsing; the lack of government regulation was a big incentive to the rapid development of this sector. No licences were required, and there was a free market. At a time when much of Mogadishu's infrastructure was disintegrating, with roads falling into disrepair, buildings shattered by bullets and shells, power lines looted and water supplies drying up, mobile phone masts started to spring up in the city. A manager at Telcom Somalia, Abdullahi Mohamed Hussein, explained why the lack of central authority made it so easy to set up a phone company: 'The government post and telecommunications company used to have a monopoly but after the regime was toppled, we were free to set up our own businesses. We saw a huge gap in the market, as all the previous services had been destroyed. There was a massive demand.'[19]

The lack of regulations and the fiercely competitive environment have helped keep prices low; Somalia has one of the cheapest mobile phone services in Africa, with telecommunications companies offering a variety of packages to phone relatives abroad for little more than the cost of a local phone call. Phone services are reliable; it is often easier to get through to a remote location in Somalia than to a sophisticated capital city elsewhere in Africa. There is also an amazing array of mobile phone handsets on offer in Somalia; some take two SIM cards at the same time; there are large phones that look the same as those used for landlines but are in fact powerful mobile phones for use in offices, homes and other fixed locations.

Somalia's strong oral culture has played a role in driving the telecommunications sector; the sound of the voice is very important in Somalia, hence the appeal of the telephone and the radio. Some of my Somali friends and colleagues seem to want everyone around them to hear both sides of their phone conversations; when they make calls, they turn on the speakerphone and, from several paces back, shout into the phone at the person on the other end, whose replies can be heard by everybody within hearing distance.

The long years of war and the resulting displacement of the Somalis to all corners of the globe mean that fast and reliable phone, Internet and money transfer services are crucial; conflict has been a key driver of these sectors. Somalis need to be connected electronically to conduct business, to keep in touch with their friends and relatives, and to know what is happening in Somalia. They are often extremely adept at using the latest technology, and have shown me all sorts of cunning tricks for using the Internet and mobile phones.

Somaliland

When most people think about Somalia, they think of unending conflict, hunger, piracy and al-Qaeda-linked violence. There is, however, another story, as Mark Bradbury explains:

Located on the northern edge of the Horn of Africa, Somaliland has emerged as one of the most stable polities in the Horn, and by 2006 could boast a popularly elected government and a political system with democratic credentials to rival any in the region and most Muslim states. As such, Somaliland challenges the image of war, disaster and social regression that has been associated with this part of Africa since the early 1990s.[20]

Ali Mazrui says there are in effect two Somalias:

After Northern Somalia's withdrawal from the Union in 1991, the Horn of Africa experienced a 'Tale of Two Somalias'. The Somalia of Mogadishu continued to be a case of anarchy without order, while the Somalia of Hargeisa was gathering momentum as a case of 'bottom-up nation-building', rooted in culture and energised from within.[21]

Visiting the 'Two Somalias' in a single day is quite an experience. The 'Somalia of Mogadishu' is not a relaxing place to be; the city is heavily militarized and divided, its front lines constantly changing. Civilians are never safe, even from the African Union peacekeepers, who have been accused by human rights groups of firing heavy artillery into residential areas. People's behaviour is severely restricted. They cannot move freely; in areas controlled by Islamist insurgents, women have to cover themselves completely, their children at risk of being forcibly recruited by al-Shabaab and other militias.

The 'other Somalia' is a world apart. In 2011, I took the plane from Mogadishu to Somaliland's port town of Berbera, where I took a walk on the beach. There I saw a group of young women frolicking in the sea, rolling about in the water, kicking their legs in the air, giggling, laughing and shrieking in delight. It was as if a lid had been taken off a pot of boiling water; people were allowed to breathe and express themselves freely. Unlike in 'the Somalia of Mogadishu', there were no African Union peacekeepers, there was just peace. There was no need for armed escorts and the only people I saw carrying guns were members of the security forces. This was a significant change from when I had previously visited Somaliland in the mid-1990s, when most young men carried weapons, as if they would feel naked without one.

In the late 1980s and early 1990s, Somaliland was probably the most comprehensively destroyed part of Somali territory. The contrast between that shattered place and the situation in 2011 was almost unbelievable. I stood on a hill overlooking the city; there were buildings as far as my eyes could see, in every direction. It felt safe on the streets; there were traffic jams, people pushed wheelbarrows loaded with Somaliland shillings, women carried small quantities of fruit for sale on brightly coloured plastic trays – everybody seemed to be doing business. There were used car lots, someone had set up a library, and there were pavement cafés for every type of Somalilander. There were teashops for those who had stayed behind during the war, for those who had returned from Ethiopia, and for others from farther afield. One café was frequented by Somalilanders based in Canada, referred to locally as 'the Canadians', another by 'the Australians', 'the Swedes', 'the Danes' and 'the British'. There were also separate teashops for people who had fled the violence in Mogadishu and elsewhere in Somalia.

People returning from the diaspora, with their knowledge, experience and resources, are behind much of the change in Somaliland. With their sense of adventure and can-do attitude, I came to think of them as the 'Somaliland Pioneers'. They help drive the economy and play a crucial role in politics; the government elected in 2010 has been accused of being too 'foreign' because so many senior positions are occupied by people from the diaspora. One 'Somaliland Pioneer', the hotelier Abdulkader

Hashi Elmi, who returned home after many years working in the oil industry in Kuwait, described how he and his friends came to the aid of Somaliland's government shortly after the territory declared independence:

> When I returned to Somaliland, everyone was carrying a gun. The territory was at the bottom of its lowest career. There was a government in name but physically there was nothing. So we had to do something. We supported the police by paying their salaries, buying them food and fuel for their cars. We did the same for judges, clerics and teachers. When our second president, Mohamed Ibrahim Egal, came to power in 1993, there was no stationery in his office, not even a pen. I went back to Kuwait and I told my fellow Somalilanders there that there was not a single pen or piece of paper on the desk of the president. Within two weeks we had filled one of the rooms in my house with stationery, which we then sent to President Egal in Hargeisa.

The 'Somaliland Pioneers' are constantly seeking to expand their business interests, while simultaneously helping to develop the territory. Abdulkader Hashi Elmi showed me a survey he and a group of other businesspeople had commissioned for a road they wanted to build leading directly north from Hargeisa to the sea, opening up a remote, inaccessible part of the territory:

> The people in that region have a problem communicating with the rest of Somaliland. The land is very fertile, there is a lot of livestock and the sea is rich in fish. But the area is cut off by a range of rugged hills which prevent people from transporting their goods for sale in Hargeisa and other towns. They desperately need a road. We can't wait until the government has enough money to build the road; the money has to come from us. Once we finish the survey, we will go to the communities

in that region and ask them to contribute whatever they can towards the road. A dollar, a sheep, anything.

Those who don't recognize Somaliland don't know us. Somaliland will continue to exist and will continue to rise up whether we are recognized or not. One of the advantages of not being recognized is that we have to depend on ourselves. We are like a tortoise. We move very slowly but we know where we are going.

A similar project has already been completed in the north-western town of Burao, where a bridge had been built across a wide river bed that in the dry season reveals the rusting remains of armoured personnel carriers and other military vehicles abandoned during the civil war, but in the rainy season becomes a raging torrent, which used to divide the town, sweeping away people and livestock who tried to cross it. The bridge has been built with private money, most of it contributed by big businesses, including the Dahabshiil money transfer company, but also by the local community, who stood to benefit from its construction. People contributed what they could: their time, their expertise, a few Somaliland shillings, a chicken, a goat or a camel.

It was in Abdulkader Hashi Elmi's hotel that I met several other 'Pioneers', people young and old who had returned to Somaliland from Malaysia, Canada, Norway, Sweden, Britain, the Gulf and other parts of the world. There were eager young computer whizz-kids excited about the many business opportunities the territory had to offer, there was a young intellectual who wanted to set up a think tank, and a petroleum engineer who had come from Norway to explore the possibility of drilling for oil.

One evening, I met a 'Canadian' Somalilander, Abdullah Farah, who told me he had started the first ever dairy farm in Somaliland. Given that the environment was so dry and arid, I told him I did not believe him. He offered to take me to the farm, so we set off early the next day, driving at great speed over uneven sandy terrain, rushing past camels, anthills and thorn trees. Suddenly, like a mirage in the desert, there appeared a patch of brilliant green. This was the 'Green Valley Dairy Farm', where a modern irrigation system has enabled Abdullah Farah to grow different varieties of grass, legumes and other food for his dairy cows, experimenting with seeds he has brought from Kenya and Sudan. The black and white Holstein cattle, which would look more at home in the green pastures of Europe, were brought by land from Ethiopia, and artificially inseminated with semen imported from the United States. The equipment in the high-tech, sparkling-clean milking parlour comes from France.

When I asked Abdullah Farah, who had no previous experience of farming, how he knew how to irrigate the land, dig wells, make silage and run a dairy farm, he roared with laughter, saying he had learned most of it from the Internet. His response embodied the wild pioneering spirit of the Somalilanders. He said the idea of starting a dairy farm came to him when his father started to suffer from brittle bones owing to a lack of calcium, a common problem in Somaliland. He said his main motivation was to improve the health of people in the territory by providing them with cows' milk; it is also possible that Abdullah Farah will make a lot of money from his dairy farm adventure.

Other Somalilanders are motivated by a more purely social conscience. Aden Ismail, who works as a psychiatrist in Canada, gives up weeks of his time for free every year to treat mental patients in Somaliland because there are no psychiatrists in the territory. The former wife of President Egal, Edna Adan Ismail, a trained midwife, retired from her job with the United Nations and built a maternity hospital in Hargeisa, where she also trains midwives:

I had dreamed of building a hospital since I was eleven years old. I started to build one in Mogadishu but it was destroyed when the conflict broke out. As I approached retirement age, I decided to have another go, this time in my native Somaliland. I was given a large patch of land on what used to be a grave-yard, a rubbish dump and later an execution ground, where they would shoot political prisoners. People hated this place but now they love it. I used my retirement benefits and other assets to build this hospital. I would much rather do that than settle somewhere else and play bridge till I am blue in the face.

While all these private initiatives are going on, the government of Somaliland remains small and weak. Because the territory is not internationally recognized, it cannot access big foreign loans for infrastructural and other developments, something that frustrates the president, Ahmed Silanyo:

We need foreign recognition because that is the only way we will become a fully fledged member of the international community. We cannot attend conferences organized by the United Nations and other organizations. We cannot benefit from programmes of the World Bank and other international bodies. We miss out on a lot by not being recognized. We have been very patient about this and we hope our patience will be rewarded very soon. If we are granted international recognition during my presidency, we would put on the biggest celebration the world has ever seen.

Somalilanders seem to be doing very well without attending international conferences or in other ways being part of the aid system. They are united and energized by their obsession with gaining international recognition; they are not content to keep operating, against the many odds, as a functioning society in an unrecognized territory. It is possible that if it were recognized,

Somaliland might start to fracture and waste money on the trappings of statehood. It might, for example, feel it has to open a grand embassy in a posh part of London instead of the single room it currently occupies in a tatty business centre in a run-down part of the East End of town. Bradbury says there are many sides to the issue of whether or not Somaliland would benefit from more outside assistance:

> Because of the disastrous military and humanitarian intervention in the south, an argument has been made that Somaliland benefited from being an 'aid free zone'. A counter-argument could be made that the international community missed the opportunity to build on the political consensus in Somaliland to reinforce principles of good governance. If limited international assistance to Somaliland did delay the physical, economic and political recovery of the country, then it had human costs. These are impossible to compute. Yet the lack of substantial foreign engagement did enable local political processes to take their course without being shaped by external resources and agendas.[22]

Somaliland has reason to believe it has the right to independence. According to the African Union, countries must stick to the boundaries they were given at independence; the British former protectorate of Somaliland was for a few days an independent country with a clearly defined border before it united with what had been the Italian colony of *Somalia Italiana* to the south. However, the unswerving resistance to Somaliland's independence by the transitional government in Mogadishu remains a major sticking point. Foreign governments have in recent years shifted their previously intransigent position towards Somaliland; the United States announced in 2010 that it would give more support to the territory. Britain has also changed its approach. Most countries argue that it is up to the African Union to decide what happens to Somaliland. Given the inefficient and largely ineffective nature of the organization, Somalilanders are unlikely to see a change in their status any time soon.

The reason why so many Somalilanders have returned home and have been able to embark on such exciting projects for themselves and for the territory as a whole is that, unlike Somalia, Somaliland has since 1991 been rebuilding its economy, society and government. It has been doing this slowly, in its own way, with a careful progression from a clan-based political system to what should ultimately be a Somali-style multiparty democracy. Because Western models of peacemaking and state-building have not been imposed from the outside, Somaliland has in many ways saved itself from the fate of Somalia. The example of Somaliland has demonstrated that, when left to themselves, Somalis can form a viable nation-state.

After breaking away from Somalia on 18 May 1991, and therefore loosening themselves from outside interference, the people of Somaliland looked deep into their own traditions, building a system which was initially based on clan politics and respect for elders but over time incorporated more modern political institutions and processes. A series of inter-clan conferences were held, where representatives from all parts of society discussed, debated and argued about what kind of political system they should have, and how power should be apportioned. Unlike the numerous foreign-sponsored 'peace conferences' organized for Somalia since 1991, these grassroots meetings organized by Somalis for Somalis came up with a system that was realistic and relevant, and has actually worked in practice. The political meetings culminated in the Boroma conference of 1993, which lasted for four months, and ended with the appointment of Somaliland's second and longest-serving president, Mohamed Ibrahim Egal. For Bradbury, the significance of this gathering stretched far beyond the borders of Somaliland: 'The 1993 Boroma conference was not only a defining political event in Somaliland, but also an example of an indigenous popular peacemaking process that has few parallels in contemporary Africa.'[23] Bradbury says the key to Somaliland's success is that, in diametric opposition to the case of Somalia, the state has grown up from the roots of society: 'If we return to Luling's description of Somalia in the 1980s as a state "suspended above a society that would never have produced it and did not demand it", Somaliland, by contrast, appears to be rooted in a popular consciousness and embedded in society rather than imposed from above.'[24]

A hybrid system of government was designed, whereby Western-style institutions were fused with more traditional forms of social and political organization. Somaliland's legislature reflects the mix of the traditional with the modern; the Senate consists of traditional clan elders while the House of Representatives is made up of elected representatives. By incorporating the traditional Somali council of elders or *guurti* into the structure of government, and giving it clearly defined roles, including the management of internal conflicts, Somaliland has built on existing forms of governance instead of ignoring or eliminating them. By amalgamating the council of elders into its political system, good use has been made of those most respected in society for their expertise in conflict resolution, and this is one of the reasons why the territory's complex internal conflicts have seldom erupted into full-scale clan warfare. As well as admitting the most respected members of society into the very heart of government, the political system has been carefully designed to reflect the clan make-up of the country. Government is essentially a power-sharing coalition of the territory's main clans, with seats in the upper and lower houses allocated according to a predetermined formula.

In order for Somaliland's hybrid political system to succeed and later to develop into a more plural system of government, it needed strong and confident leadership. This was especially true during the fragile early period, when it was a fledgling self-declared republic and civil war was raging in Somalia, which was extremely hostile to the secession. The man who had the nerve to steer Somaliland through its infant years was President Egal, an experienced and charismatic politician, whose personality was crucial to the territory's survival and success. He knew how to stand up to his critics at home and abroad. He could survive the wild world of Somali politics, having served in several powerful positions, including that of prime minister, as well as spending time in prison under Siad Barre. He was wily and irreverent, with a bold sense of humour. He was not one to stand on ceremony; when I met him during a particularly difficult period in 1994, with an enemy militia on the outskirts of the capital and clan fighting in other parts of Somaliland, he exuded a devil-may-care attitude, appearing to will his enemies away by confidence alone.

Egal lasted long enough to carry Somaliland into the world, and to give its population the confidence that they could go it alone. When he died in 2002 Somaliland had existed for eleven years and had by that time developed into a viable entity, with hundreds of thousands of refugees who had fled the war of the 1980s returning home to make decent lives for themselves. The transition to a new presidency was relatively smooth, partly because there was a clear method for selecting a successor, which was one of the key roles given to the elders in the upper house.

It was with the appointment of Dahir Riyale Kahin as president that the territory entered the second stage of its political development, making a fairly smooth transition to limited multiparty democracy. Somaliland adopted the 'tortoise' approach to political plurality, slow but sure. For the first twelve years of its existence, there were no political parties at all. Then, in order to prevent political organizations from becoming too closely identified with clan interests, the number of parties was limited to three; Kulmiye, the Unity of Democrats (UDUB) and the Justice and

Development party. The constitution forbids the parties from forming along clan or regional lines. By 2011, discussions were under way for the creation of a more plural political system. This pattern is in many ways similar to that of Uganda, where President Yoweri Museveni initially imposed a no-party system, which was gradually allowed to develop into multiparty democracy as the country emerged from years of conflict and political brutality. The Ugandan experiment was initially quite successful, but eventually became corrupted as Museveni clung on to power.

The government of Somaliland has at times been accused by human rights groups of intolerance and repression. In July 2007, the leaders of a fledgling political group, Qaran, were arrested, accused by the interior ministry of threatening national security. Three of Qaran's leaders were later imprisoned without trial.

In the presidential elections of April 2003, Dahir Riyale won by the slimmest of margins, with just eighty votes more than his main rival from the Kulmiye party. Despite allegations of vote rigging and political misdemeanour, Somaliland did not descend into chaos and bloodshed. Riyale remained as head of state for a second term. There have been raging debates in parliament, and the occasional fist fight, but Somaliland has managed to keep a lid on political disputes, suggesting it is developing into a healthy, robust democracy, where difference of opinion does not mean war.

There was a period of great political tension from 2008 to 2010 when elections were repeatedly delayed owing to problems with the voters' list and other complications. When the election was eventually held in 2010, the population was determined to vote, queuing for hours in the hot sun, ignoring threats from al-Shabaab that they should not participate in the election. The opposition Kulmiye party candidate, Ahmed Silanyo, won by a narrow margin. Unlike the leaders of more advanced African democracies, such as Côte d'Ivoire Zimbabwe and Kenya, the incumbent president accepted the result, and handed over power to Silanyo, the territory's fourth president in twenty years.

Somaliland is not without its problems; the provinces of Sool, Sanaag and Cayn are under dispute with Puntland, with clashes breaking out intermittently between the two sides. Also present in these provinces is the SSC rebel group, which is fighting to reunite the area with Somalia as a whole. Somaliland has also encountered Islamist violence; the leader of al-Shabaab, Ahmed Abdi Godane, is a Somalilander, and the security services say there are al-Shabaab sleeper cells in the territory. In October 2008 al-Shabaab carried out three simultaneous suicide bombings in Hargeisa, attacking the presidential palace, the headquarters of the United Nations Development Programme, and the Ethiopian liaison office. At the same time, it carried out two attacks in Puntland. A total of about thirty people were killed.

A senior official in Somaliland's security department told me that the police and military in the territory are weak and unable to cope with serious threats to security. He said the security forces were corrupt: 'the law here is fifty US dollars'. He described Hargeisa as 'a gateway to Mogadishu', with some Islamist extremists entering the region via Somaliland, where they were less likely to be treated with suspicion. The official told me another problem was the presence in Somaliland of young Somalis who had been in trouble with the law, especially drugs, in the UK, Holland, Denmark and other European countries. He said they melted into the local population, bringing crime to the territory.

The story of the 'two Somalias' throws up some important questions. Why, after more than twenty years, do the United Nations and the world's most powerful countries continue to fund, recognize and support the 'central' government in Mogadishu, whose power has at times failed to reach beyond a few districts of the capital, and has never extended to the whole of Somalia? Why have they been so slow to learn from the example of Somaliland,

7 Women police officers in Somaliland (Mary Harper)

and realize that less rather than more outside interference might be the best answer? With the UK and the USA now giving more support to Somaliland and other relatively stable Somali regions, there is the added danger that throwing money at the territories might lead to new problems.

Somaliland is already awash with non-governmental organizations. As I drove through Hargeisa, most of the signs I saw, apart from the advertisements for money transfer companies and mobile phones, were announcing the presence of local and international NGOs, and UN agencies. I made a list of those I saw in just a couple of streets: Action Against Poverty, Somaliland Youth Peer Education Group, Handicap International, UNESCO, Mercy Corps, FAO, UNDP ... As I walked around the poorer parts of the city, people would stop and ask me, 'What NGO are you from? What have you brought me?' Another disturbing consequence of the increased presence of international development agencies is the 'brain drain' to such institutions of talented, educated Somalilanders from local businesses and other home-grown organizations, lured by the offer of higher salaries and perhaps the prestige of working for the UN or another international body. Several Somalilanders, who spent years rebuilding their country without much outside help, have told me that they fear the flood of NGOs into the territory could undo the 'can-do', enterprising spirit of the population, replacing it with a lazy dependency mentality.

The positive examples from Somaliland, especially the creation of a functioning political system, could serve as models for other semi-autonomous regions in Somalia, but taken too far, this could result in the formation of several Somali states, and the permanent disintegration of Somalia as a whole. Another option would be to reincorporate Somaliland into a highly federalized Somali state, with its hybrid political system used as a model for other regional administrations. This is highly unlikely, because Somaliland wants to have as little to do with Somalia as possible, at least in its current state.

A former foreign minister in the Somali transitional government, Ismail Mohamed Huure, nicknamed Booba, is originally from Somaliland, but had, when I met him in 2010, been living for several years in the Andalus Hotel in Nairobi. Although fundamentally opposed to the idea of an independent Somaliland, he suggested its capital, Hargeisa, could serve as the centre of power for the whole of Somalia:

> Somaliland is now in a position to govern the whole of Somalia. Somaliland is secure at the moment, but if the situation in Mogadishu continues, sooner or later, the violence is going to hit Hargeisa. You cannot have peace and stability in one area and not the other. Somalis are either going to suffer together or prosper together. We are one nation; clans do not make

nations. The Somali nation in the Horn of Africa is a wholly unified country. We are not looking to re-create the Somali nation from the five points of the star; that is a dream in the sky. We must look at the facts on the ground, at the two areas where you have a hundred per cent Somali population. These two regions will share a destiny together, whether it is peaceful or not.

In 2011, some members of parliament in Mogadishu and other influential Somalis from the south started muttering about the possibility of governing the whole of Somalia from Hargeisa. A few have even told me they would like Somaliland's president, Ahmed Silanyo, to take charge of all Somali territory.

As Michael Walls points out, Somalia has a lot to learn from Somaliland about how to transform itself from a war-shattered disaster to a functioning polity:

> At a time when developments in the southern and central Somali territories provide such cause for despair, it is important to recognise and attempt to learn from the different reality that pertains in Somaliland, where local resources have been effectively employed in the cause of achieving a lasting peace and what appears to be a viable system of democracy.[25]

The key to the success of Somaliland lies in the hybrid and dynamic nature of its political structures, which give room to the clans and traditional authority systems but do not allow them to dominate the political landscape. The journalist Rageh Omaar, who comes from Somaliland, finds it strange that outside powers have not engaged more fully with the territory in terms of foreign policy towards Somalia, choosing instead to focus on Somalia's other neighbours:

> The beleaguered UN-backed government in Mogadishu has no other partners with a strong security force, democratic

institutions and an intimate knowledge of Somali culture, language, clan system and politics. Up till now, the west has looked to Ethiopia, Kenya, Uganda and others to be their key allies, overlooking the one partner that has a direct interest in bringing peace and security to Mogadishu and halting the spread of nationalism.[26]

The experience of Somaliland can at the very least provide an example of hope and potential to those parts of Somalia that have failed to extract themselves from an almost endless cycle of conflict and instability. The similarities between the regions are greater than their differences; if Somaliland can do it, so can Somalia. Both have been shattered by war, both have complex and inherently divisive clan systems, and both have enterprising, bold populations. The fact that even the most violent parts of Somalia have managed to experience rapid economic growth in some sectors, including livestock, money transfer and telecommunications, suggests that state 'failure' does not mean country failure.

5 | PIRACY

My name is Gedow Ali. I live somewhere on the Somali coast, bordering the Indian Ocean. I would prefer not to be referred to as a 'pirate' but as a member of the 'Coast Guard'.

We used to live happily in our area, but circumstances forced us to become what we are now. Our livelihood as fishermen was threatened by foreigners who came to our seas and stole our fish. We decided to do something about it; that is why we formed our 'Coast Guard' group.

We 'arrest' ships that come into our waters. We charge them a 'fee' and ask them never to come back. We use this money to replace our equipment that has been destroyed by the foreign aggressors, and to compensate the families of members of our group who have been killed or injured by them. My life is very comfortable now but some people in the 'Coast Guards' live in miserable conditions.

I have heard it said that we are linked to big international criminal networks. This is completely untrue, although we would love to have the support of anybody who takes our side against the aggression of the United States.

We used to know only the whereabouts of foreign ships sailing near our shores but the aggressors have become more active in their patrols. We don't care about that, though, because we have now worked out how to find ships anywhere, even those near Oman, India and Madagascar.

The rest of the world believes we are bad people. They think we are criminals. But nobody has come to ask us for our side of the story. This situation came about because we had no choice; we were forced to become 'Coast Guards' because of the foreign aggressors. We will keep doing what we are doing until people come and talk to us, and try to understand our problems. (Gedow Ali, February 2011)

The explosion of Somali piracy since the mid-2000s has captured the world's attention more than any other aspect of life in the country. It has generated more newspaper column inches and media airtime than other subjects, even though it involves the activities of only a tiny section of the population, and gives a distorted picture of the situation in Somalia as a whole.

The Western media have an almost unquenchable thirst for pirate stories. There is something romantic and childlike about the subject, but also something brutal and violent. Tiny speedboats, with a handful of scrawny, gun-toting Somalis on board, buzz around the Indian Ocean hunting for their prey. The pirates use the most basic of equipment, such as grappling hooks, ropes and ladders, to board vast cargo ships, taking their crews hostage, and releasing them and their vessels only once multimillion-dollar ransoms are paid. There are gunfights, heroic rescue missions and tragic endings. This is the stuff of Hollywood movies and adventure stories, but it is real.[1]

A new economy has grown up around Somali piracy, which generates wealth not only for those who hijack the ships, but also for their sponsors and those who negotiate on their behalf. Others are making money from the substantial industry that has developed around trying to deal with the problem of Somali piracy. New security companies have been set up to help protect ships from the pirates. Anti-piracy equipment is being designed and sold, including electric fences, powerful hoses and cannons that beam intolerable sounds at suspected attackers as they approach their target vessel. New breeds of consultants, insurers, lawyers,

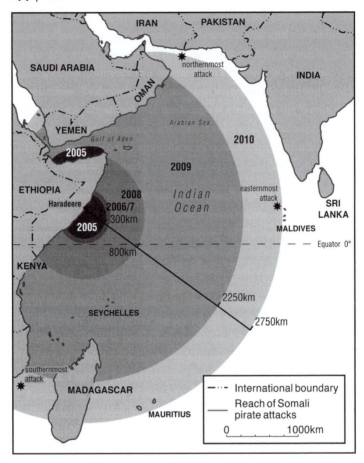

Map 4.1 Reach of Somali pirate attacks, 2005–10

counsellors, security personnel and ransom negotiators are making a good living from Somali piracy. Insurance premiums for ships sailing off the coast of Somalia increased tenfold following the rise of piracy in the area.[2]

Despite the existence of all these new specialists, and the presence of an international naval force patrolling off the coast of

Somalia, piracy in the region has increased, although the number of attacks has varied according to the season. In October 2009, eight vessels and about 170 crew members were being held by Somali pirates; by April 2011, the number had risen to about fifty vessels and more than eight hundred crew members.[3]

Somalis have become the most active and effective pirates in the world; according to the International Maritime Bureau, forty-nine of the fifty-three ships hijacked in 2010 were seized by Somali pirates. The US think tank One Earth Future calculated in 2010 that maritime piracy, most of which occurs off the coast of Somalia, was costing the global economy between seven and twelve billion dollars a year.[4]

It seems the only way to guarantee that pirates will not attack a ship sailing off the coast of Somalia is to provide it with a naval escort. This has been the case for World Food Programme ships transporting food aid to Somalia from the Kenyan port of Mombasa, and they have so far avoided attack. But it would be impossible to provide individual protection for every one of the tens of thousands of ships that pass through the area every year.

The international naval force has established a safe transit corridor in the Gulf of Aden, through which some 35 per cent of the world's oil is transported, and which became known as 'Pirate Alley' owing to the frequency of attacks. The pirates' reaction was to change their techniques; instead of setting off from Somalia in small fibreglass skiffs, they hijacked medium-sized vessels to use as 'mother ships', using them to transport their speedboats far out into the Indian Ocean, towards the Seychelles, India and Madagascar, and launching their attacks from there. By 2011, Somali pirates were operating in such an enormous area – about four million square kilometres of ocean – that it was impossible for international naval patrols to monitor them, let alone to control them. The use of 'mother ships', often operated by captured crew members, has enabled piracy to continue all year round because these larger vessels can cope with bad weather and rough seas.

The *Sirius Star*

One of the most dramatic and audacious attacks occurred in November 2008, when a small group of Somali pirates hijacked the *Sirius Star*, a gigantic Saudi-owned supertanker, the size of three football fields. It was attacked more than 450 nautical miles south-east of the Kenyan coast, and was at the time the biggest ship ever captured by pirates. The *Sirius Star*, which was sailing from Saudi Arabia to the United States, was loaded with US$100,000,000 worth of oil, more than a quarter of Saudi Arabia's daily output. News of the hijack affected global markets, precipitating an increase in the price of crude oil.

Such brazen attacks are possible because pirates can sometimes board vessels without crews even noticing; they identify the point where the ship is lowest in the water, approaching it in a tiny, fast-moving skiff, often under cover of darkness. They throw up a grappling hook and scamper up on to the ship with the help of a rope or a ladder. As the ship's crew is usually unarmed, the pirates, who carry guns, are at an advantage once they are on board.

I managed to obtain a phone number for the *Sirius Star* but every time my Somali colleagues or I got through to the ship, the pirates would cut us off as soon as we told them we were from the BBC. We tried speaking to them in English, Somali and Arabic, but got nowhere. I became so obsessed with calling the pirates that I stored their number on my mobile phone, ringing them several times a day. My daughter had seen me trying to call them. One rainy Sunday evening in London, as I was stuck in bad traffic after collecting her from a birthday party, she started pestering me, asking whether she could ring the pirates. I became exasperated and eventually gave in, tossing the phone to her in the back of the car. 'It's under "P" for Pirates,' I said. She rang the number and started chatting. A bizarre conversation ensued whereby she managed to convince the pirates to speak to me, telling them I would call the following day.

The next morning, a Somali colleague and I tried the number. The pirates were expecting our call, and asked us to ring back later to speak to their leader, who they said was asleep because he had been up all night guarding the hostages. We rang at the appointed time and were greeted by the pirate leader, who called himself 'Daybed'. He sounded relaxed and in control, and was perfectly happy to speak to us. He seemed baffled by the logbook and other items he had found on board; from the way he spoke to us, it was evident that he and his pirate gang were somewhat astonished by the enormous size of the ship they had captured.

Daybed said he was not directly involved in any of the negotiations for the release of the *Sirius Star*, and had no idea what size ransom was being demanded. He told us the only reason he had captured the oil tanker was for money, and that he would be satisfied with what he described as 'the usual asking price' for releasing a ship, which was at the time about two million dollars. He emphasized that the twenty-five Polish, Croatian, Saudi, Filipino and British crew members on board were precious cargo, and were far more valuable alive than dead: 'The members of the crew are not prisoners. They can move from place to place, wherever and whenever they want to. They can even sleep in their usual beds and we have allowed them to keep their own keys. The only thing missing is their freedom to leave the ship.'

Daybed explained that, although he understood the negative global impact of the surge of piracy off the Somali coast, he was faced with little choice:

We are fully aware of the consequences but the world needs to understand the problems we face in Somalia. There has been no peace for eighteen years. There is no life here. The last resource Somalis have is the sea, but foreign trawlers have plundered all our fish. This is what drove us to piracy. We have to engage in piracy in order to survive.

The Polish captain of the ship, Marek Nishky, was then put on the phone: 'We are generally OK. All crew and officers are in good shape. There is no reason for complaint. We have already been given the opportunity to talk to our families. As you must realise, this is the most important thing for us now.'

A ransom of US$25 million was initially demanded for the release of the *Sirius Star*, but two months after the hijacking, it was set free for a reported US$3 million. The ransom money was flown out to the supertanker in a light aircraft, which dropped the cash down in a bag attached to a small orange parachute, which floated through the air on to the deck of the ship.

The story did not end well for the pirates. According to their relatives, a storm blew up as they were making their way back to Somalia in a small boat. The vessel capsized; five of the pirates are said to have drowned, the other three making it back to shore but without their share of the ransom money, which had been washed away in the rough sea. An uncle of one of the drowned pirates said his body eventually drifted ashore, with US$153,000 in a plastic bag in his pocket, all that remained of the US$3 million ransom.[5]

Myths and misconceptions

Several myths and misconceptions surround Somali piracy; some have been created by the pirates themselves, some by the media, which often simplify and sensationalize the issue, and some by foreign security consultants and other parties who stand to benefit from the perpetuation of the problem.

One of the prevailing myths is that all pirates started life as fishermen but were forced to change careers because foreign trawlers emptied Somali waters of fish. Although Somalia's fish stock has undoubtedly been depleted by fishermen from overseas, the 'plundering by foreign trawlers' has become the standard answer used by Somali pirates to explain their actions, almost as if it offers a justification for what they do.

Like Gedow Ali, who was quoted at the beginning of this chapter, many pirates describe themselves as 'Coast Guards' protecting their coastline from foreign trawlers and ships dumping toxic waste, charging trespassers a 'fee'. The choice of language appears to be an attempt to decriminalize their activities. One pirate, who called himself 'Hassan', operated out of the port of Haradeere in central Somalia before Islamist forces took over the town in 2010:

> I used to be a fisherman but foreign trawlers came to our waters and stole all our fish. A few years ago, there were more than seven hundred foreign trawlers stealing fish from Somali waters. Now there are no fish to be found – they have left us with nothing.
>
> When they did that to us, we decided to hunt them down, and we are now reaping the benefits. We have done really well out of those foreigners who disturbed our way of life because we are now profiting from our decision to turn on them.
>
> We have decided to turn those foreigners into our fish, and we are now fishing for them. The only people doing well from 'fishing' now are us 'Coast Guards' because we are 'fishing' for hostages.

Many Somali pirates take great offence at being labelled 'pirates'. Some believe the term should be applied to foreign vessels entering Somali waters. I spoke to the pirate, or as he would put it 'Coast Guard', Dahir, in the coastal town of Hobyo in July 2011:

> I have a question for the world. Who is a pirate? Is it the trawlers and warships who have arrived in our seas and taken

everything from us, our fish, our resources, our freedom, everything? Or is it us, the people who are guarding our coasts? That is the question I have for the international community. That is the question that has to be answered.

The authorities in Somalia have, at times, contributed to the myth that what is happening off the coast of Somalia does not amount to piracy. In January 2011 the Somali parliament refused to pass a bill that would make piracy illegal. Some MPs described the pirates as 'heroes' for keeping foreign fishing fleets away from Somali waters; they said they were not pirates, but unofficial coastguards. Media reports have also suggested that pirates are modern-day 'Robin Hoods', stealing from the rich to give to the poor when, in reality, it would be more accurate to describe them as criminals. One pirate, Adan, was more frank about his motivations than many of his colleagues: 'Pirates are all bad. They are groups of people that agree on just to rob ships at sea.'[6]

In his study of Somali piracy, the Norwegian academic Stig Jarle Hansen makes the point that if the sole mission of the pirates or 'Coast Guards' was to clear Somali waters of illegal trawlers, they would attack foreign fishing boats, not cargo ships, yachts and oil tankers:

> While it is highly likely that pirates actually do prevent illegal fishing by scaring foreign trawlers, the pirates' targets clearly indicate that profit considerations are more important than any agenda to protect against illegal fishing. The ships captured by pirates are generally not trawlers fishing illegally, but ordinary cargo ships and bulk carriers just passing through Somali, Yemeni or international waters.[7]

In some cases, instead of clearing the sea of foreign trawlers and allowing Somalis to fish in peace, pirates have prevented local fishermen from working. Sometimes they scare them away, some-

8 Somali pirate, Ismail Elixh (Mary Harper)

times international naval patrols and other ships mistake Somali fishermen for pirates, firing powerful hoses at them, confiscating their equipment, arresting them, or otherwise disrupting their activities. In other instances, the lure of hefty ransoms proves too much for the fishermen, who quit their original jobs to become pirates themselves. Reports from pirate villages describe fishing boats left disintegrating on the beaches, abandoned by their former owners, who now take to the sea in modern speedboats, hunting for hostages rather than fish. In Hargeisa prison, I met a captured pirate, Ismail Elixh, who told me how one day he decided to stop being a fisherman, went to his local market in Bossasso, Puntland, and bought an AK-47, a bazooka and a speedboat. He was caught on his first pirate expedition and sentenced to fifteen years in jail. He showed no regret for his actions, despite the fact that he had completely lost touch with his family and would spend years of his life in prison in what was essentially a foreign territory.

Pirate economy

Piracy has become so lucrative, with millions of dollars paid for the release of ships and their crew, that over time it has attracted many non-fishermen, developing into a more sophisticated criminal enterprise. However, fishermen remain an essential part of any pirate gang because of their knowledge of the sea and their ability to operate boats and other maritime equipment. With its potentially massive rewards, piracy has become an attractive career option. It served the pirate Hassan well: 'My financial situation is very, very good. I don't even need to go to sea this year because I seized a ship last year. I have invested the money I made from this very wisely indeed. I am doing absolutely fine. My life is much better than when I was a fisherman.'

Although tens of millions of dollars are paid in ransoms every year, it is impossible to work out exactly how much money is made by those involved in Somali piracy and how it is distributed. Tracing ransom payments is made more difficult by the fact that Somalis have an age-old system of dealing with money, known as *hawala*, which is based on trust and verbal communication, and often leaves neither a paper nor an electronic trail.

The head of the East African Seafarers' Assistance Programme, Andrew Mwangura, monitors piracy off the Somali coast and has negotiated with pirates. He has sent me text messages telling me exactly where and when a ship has been hijacked, hours before the incident is picked up by news agencies. He says the pirates who engage in the actual hijackings do not get all the proceeds from the ransom payments: 'They are the foot soldiers. They are young men, often teenagers, and they certainly don't end up with all the money.'[8]

A mini-economy has developed around piracy, benefiting people living in coastal villages in north-east and central Somalia as well as those farther afield. There does not appear to be any universal set of rules for how the money is divided, and any information about this subject should be treated with caution because of the reluctance of those involved in such criminal activity to disclose concrete or specific details. This breakdown of the distribution of ransom payments was presented in a United Nations report based on information gathered from pirates in the north-eastern village of Eyl in the semi-autonomous region of Puntland, which was for a time a major pirate base:

- Maritime militia (pirates involved in the actual hijacking) – 30 per cent
- Ground militia (armed groups who control the territory where the pirates are based) – 10 per cent
- Local community (elders and local officials) – 10 per cent
- Financier – 20 per cent
- Sponsor – 30 per cent

Farah Ismail Eid, who was sentenced to fifteen years in prison for piracy, gave a slightly different picture of how the money is distributed:

- Maritime militia (pirates involved in the actual hijacking) – 30 per cent
- Pirate leader – 20 per cent
- Investments for future missions, including guns, fuel and cigarettes – 20 per cent
- Government officials – 30 per cent[9]

The first pirate to board a hijacked vessel is said to receive either double the share of money or a vehicle; the others get equal amounts. If a pirate is killed or injured, his family will be given some form of financial compensation.

There have been allegations of government officials receiving a cut from piracy, especially in Puntland, where pirates have been reported to make more money from ransom payments every year than the annual budget of the region, which is about US$20 million. The director general of the ministry of fisheries and ports, Abdi Waheed Johar, acknowledged in 2008 that 'there are government people working with pirates'.[10] The deputy chief of Puntland's police force was sacked owing to his alleged involvement in piracy. A report by a UN monitoring group said in 2010 that

> After twelve years of relatively positive evolution in Puntland, the newly established administration of Abdirahman Mohamed 'Faroole' is nudging Puntland in the direction of becoming a criminal state. Monitoring Group investigations, involving interviews with sources possessing first-hand knowledge of piracy operations, ransom negotiations and/or payments have confirmed that senior Puntland officials, including President Faroole and members of his cabinet, notably the minister of the interior, General Abdullahi Ahmed Jama 'Ilkajiir' and the minister for internal security, General Abdillahi Sa'iid Samatar, have received proceeds from piracy and/or kidnapping.[11]

Money from ransom payments trickles down to people living in pirate villages. A woman in the former pirate stronghold of Haradeere, Shamso Moalim, described how piracy had changed things for her family: 'Regardless of how the money is coming in, legally or illegally, I can say it has started a life in our town. Our children are not worrying about food now. They go to Islamic schools in the morning and play football in the afternoon. They are happy.'[12]

Residents of pirate villages have described how every time a hijacked ship is anchored in the bay, the pirates come ashore to buy fuel, water, soft drinks, sheep, goats, rice, spaghetti and cigarettes. A shopkeeper in Haradeere, Sahra Sheikh Dahir, said, 'the pirates depend on us, and we benefit from them'.[13] Another source of income for people in areas controlled by pirates is the preparation and sale of special food for the hostages, who often do not appreciate Somali cuisine.

Lifestyle

Much has been said about how piracy has brought glamour and wealth to people's lives, and to their coastal villages. However, as pirates are often forced to move base, the villages have remained dusty and scruffy, with most of the new money invested in regional capitals and other large towns. The proceeds from Somali piracy are reported to have contributed to the phenomenal development of commercial and other property in the mainly Somali Eastleigh district of Nairobi, and the cash purchase by Somalis of expensive houses in luxury districts of the city. The Somali community in Kenya has vigorously denied this.

The property boom in Puntland's regional capital, Garowe, and its main port town of Bossasso can be more clearly linked to piracy. Large new villas, or 'palaces' as Somalis call them, have been built, surrounded by high walls. Some pirates are keen on conspicuous consumption and fast living, with a taste for flashy cars and expensive Land Cruisers. Somali men complain that the surge in piracy has inflated the price of marriage, with pirates paying large dowries for new wives, holding wedding parties that last for days, with the best music, food and other treats on offer. Many people have told me that pirates are addicted to alcohol, qat and hard drugs, corrupting the communities in which they live. This may be another part of the 'pirate myth', and a way for Somalis not involved in piracy to distance themselves from the activity.

Apart from the fast cars, new houses and lavish wedding parties, some of the money is reinvested in piracy itself. The pirates have graduated from being simple fishermen with rickety boats and a couple of rusty guns into high-tech operators armed with modern weapons, travelling in expensive vessels. One reason why the pirates can operate hundreds of kilometres out to sea is that they can afford satellite tracking systems and faster, more robust boats. Despite the existence of a UN arms embargo against

Somalia, the pirates have had no trouble in getting their hands on large quantities of arms and ammunition. After two decades of civil conflict, the country is awash with weapons. Guns, fuel and other essential piracy equipment are available in Yemen, a relatively short distance across the Gulf of Aden. The longer piracy goes on, the more experienced they will become, devising ever more ingenious ways of seizing enormous ships, their crews and their precious cargoes.

Structure

The growing sophistication of Somali piracy has led to suggestions that it has become a highly complex operation, linked to international criminal gangs. In February 2011, the head of the United States counter-piracy network, Donna Lee Hopkins, said Somali piracy has been completely transformed over the years. 'Somali piracy has grown from being essentially a garden-variety, local, off-the-coast protest against illegal fishing ... into a seriously networked and capable, transnational, organised and criminal enterprise.'[14]

She said regional instability and a critical trade route have combined to create a 'perfect storm' for Somali piracy, warning that it risked becoming an insurmountable problem. Her description differs radically from that of Stig Jarle Hansen, who argues that Somali pirates are organized into simpler, smaller, local units:

> The myths of piracy in the greater Gulf of Aden are many, but the average pirate group is a clan-based, low-tech group, consisting of former fishermen. Pirates are thus decentralized, and far from the advanced structures suggested by many observers. The investor structure behind them resembles Somali investor structures around the world.[15]

Hansen suggests pirates are organized informally, and that a 'pirate group' sometimes represents no more than a family unit:

Each pirate group is usually a loose constellation around a pirate leader who is usually a veteran pirate, reinvesting funds in new pirate missions, who often functions as a fund raiser … Groups vary in complexity from a single subsistence group that consists of a father, a son and a single skiff, to larger groups of up to 200 individuals.[16]

Despite what Hansen describes as the relatively informal nature of pirate gangs, interviews I conducted in 2011 with members of several different pirate groups suggest they have strict written codes of conduct. The rules varied according to the group. They included rules for treating hostages and different procedures for attacking ships, with some, especially those for South Korean vessels, allowing for more violent forms of aggression. As one pirate, Dahir, told me: 'We have different sets of rules for different countries. For example, if we encounter a South Korean ship we attack it in a violent way. It all depends on how the foreign ships treat us. The South Koreans and Indians treat us more violently than others, so we treat them brutally in return.'

All pirate groups had sanctions against members who broke the rules, including imprisonment, fines and expulsion from the group. Those who followed the rules most faithfully were rewarded, usually with respect, but sometimes with gifts or financial incentives.[17]

Links with radical Islamists

Some media and other reports have said pirates are linked to al-Shabaab and other radical groups, serving as an important source of finance for the Islamist insurgencies. It is likely that pirates have paid fees to Islamist groups controlling areas they operate in, but the relationship does not appear to go any farther.

The only time Somali piracy has been brought under control was in 2006 when the Union of Islamic Courts (UIC) held power in much of southern and central Somalia. The UIC stated that piracy was *haraam*, or against the principles of Islam, launching attacks against pirate ports, and succeeding in virtually eliminating piracy from the country. Another Islamist group which took on the pirates was Hizbul Islam. In 2010 it drove the pirates from one of their main strongholds in Haradeere, accusing them of being un-Islamic. There were dramatic reports of some three to four hundred pirates fleeing through the bush with their weapons, some on foot, others in Land Cruisers. They later settled in the port of Hobyo to the north of Haradeere. As long as the situation in Somalia remains fluid and unstable, it is likely that the pirates will always be able to find a base somewhere along the country's long stretch of coastline.

The best option?

World powers were caught by surprise when piracy first started in Somalia. There was no mechanism available to deal effectively with the problem, meaning the pirates could operate with little risk and the potential of high reward. The commander of the United States Navy's fifth fleet, Vice-Admiral William Gortney, recognized why piracy was so attractive to Somalis: 'There is no reason not to be a pirate. The vessel I am trying to pirate, they won't shoot at me, I am going to get my money. They won't arrest me because there is no place to try me.'[18] Vice-Admiral Gortney's perspective is shared by Patrick Cullen, a security expert at the London School of Economics: 'Piracy is an excellent business model if you operate from an impoverished, lawless place like Somalia. The risk–reward ratio is huge.'[19]

Piracy has been directly and indirectly assisted by foreign aid. Poverty alleviation projects in coastal areas have in all likelihood provided fishing boats that were not used for their intended purpose; the improvement of infrastructure, such as piers, may also have helped. One of the best-known examples of how well-intentioned foreign assistance can end up helping the wrong people was in Puntland, where the British company Hart Security

UK provided local coastguards with training, boats and other equipment to help them patrol the sea for pirates and illegal foreign trawlers. Although the project was initially quite successful, Hart pulled out of the area in the early 2000s following the outbreak of a local conflict. Many of the well-trained new 'coastguards' swiftly changed jobs, becoming pirates, and putting their new equipment and expertise to completely the opposite use to that for which it had originally been intended.

What do you do with a pirate when you catch one?

One of the main problems surrounding Somali piracy has been working out what to do with pirates once they are caught. The UN Convention on the Law of the Sea defines piracy as a universal crime and gives sovereign nations the right to seize and prosecute pirates. But many countries have lacked the specific laws to deal with them. There has also been confusion about which country should assert its jurisdiction; a ship might fly one flag, belong to another country, hold cargo destined for several places, and have a crew made up of many different nationalities. The nationality of the warship seizing the suspected pirates is also relevant.

Initially, most of the pirates caught by foreign warships were simply set free. Many countries involved in the international naval patrols followed a 'catch and release' policy, with the aim of disrupting the pirates rather than going through the complicated process of putting them on trial. In September 2008, for example, a Danish warship captured ten suspected pirates cruising along the Gulf of Aden with rocket-propelled grenades and a long ladder. After holding them for a week, the Danes concluded they did not have the jurisdiction to prosecute them, so they confiscated their equipment, took them to the coast of Somalia and dumped them on a beach. In April 2009, Dutch forces serving with a NATO patrol force caught seven Somali pirates but let them go with their boat and enough supplies to ensure they made it safely back home. NATO's maritime spokesman, Commander Chris Davies, said that legally there was no other option: 'It is a matter of legislation. The pirates were initially detained and had the arms taken off them and immobilized. The pirates have been sent back in their skiff, and given food and provisions.'[20]

Other pirates have not been so lucky. Some have been handed over to the authorities in Puntland where they are locked up in overcrowded jails. One spent seven months on board an American warship because nobody could decide what to do with him. Others, captured by Yemeni patrols, have been tried in that country and sentenced to death.

As time went on, some of the pirates were taken to prisons in France, the Netherlands, the USA and elsewhere, some waiting months to go on trial as the relevant legislation was prepared. The first case to go to trial in Europe opened in a Dutch court in May 2010. Sitting in a Rotterdam courtroom, 'dressed in borrowed clothes and looking variously confused, bored and cheerful',[21] five Somali suspects were prosecuted under 'sea robbery' laws originally drafted in the seventeenth century. The suspects said they had been fishing and had not fired any shots. However, Turkish crew members, who had been on board a Dutch Antilles registered cargo ship, testified that the men had approached the vessel at great speed, firing their guns and launching a rocket at the ship's bridge. The Somalis were found guilty and each sentenced to five years in jail.

The first people to be convicted of piracy by a United States jury since 1820 were five Somalis who in March 2011 were sentenced to life imprisonment. They had made the fatal error of mistaking a US navy ship on an anti-piracy mission for a merchant vessel.

Western countries fear that when pirates complete their prison sentences they will try to claim asylum. The pirates in detention in Holland were said to be very happy; for the first time in their lives they had flushing toilets, twenty-four-hour electricity and comfortable mattresses. A lawyer representing one of the pirates explained the relative luxury of life inside a Dutch prison: 'When I first spoke to my client, he said being here was like heaven. For the first time in his life he didn't feel he was in danger, and he was in a modern prison with the first modern toilet and shower that he had ever had.'[22] As well as experiencing the relative comfort of five years in a Dutch prison, in a private cell with a television, toilet and shower, the pirates will in all likelihood be eligible to apply for asylum once their sentences are completed.

By March 2011, more than eight hundred Somali pirates were in prison in sixteen different countries. There have been various efforts to coordinate the trials and imprisonment of the pirates, but so far none of them has proved satisfactory. In 2009, the United States, the European Union, Canada and other countries reached an agreement with Kenya whereby pirate suspects would be transferred to the coastal town of Mombasa for detention and trial. However, in April 2010 the Kenyan authorities said they would not accept any more piracy suspects as they lacked the financial resources to deal with them. They said the country's judicial system was already strained, and hinted that they did not want Kenya to become the 'Pirate Guantánamo'. More foreign funds were then allocated for a special pirate court in Mombasa, but so far the arrangement has not proved satisfactory.

In 2010, the Seychelles, which has been badly affected by Somali piracy, signed an agreement with the United Nations to prosecute suspected pirates. However, the islands have only one prison and are not sufficiently equipped to deal with the problem on a large scale. There have also been initiatives to set up internationally funded pirate courts and prisons in Somaliland and Puntland, but at the time of writing, these too were beset by difficulties.

The longer it goes on ...

As the pursuit of pirates off the coast of Somalia becomes more aggressive, and as more pirates are sentenced to prison, the nature of piracy is becoming more violent. It was initially extremely rare for hostages to be killed or injured, as, for the pirates, they were worth far more alive than dead. However, a growing number of captives have died in recent years. In February 2011, four American hostages were killed during a rescue operation by US forces. The fragile status quo, whereby ships and their crew were returned once ransoms were paid, and pirates captured by international naval patrols released and allowed to go home, has been threatened. As growing numbers of pirates are killed by private security forces or naval commandos storming ships, it is likely that violence towards hostages will increase.

Pirates have also become violent when ransom negotiations drag on or fail to proceed smoothly. In January 2010, 'Adowe', one of the pirates holding the British couple Paul and Rachel Chandler, told me how what he described as the 'junior' members of his gang had 'pointed their guns at the couple and hit them' because they were 'so frustrated by the lack of progress in the ransom negotiations'.

A report published by the One Earth Future Foundation in 2011 explodes the myth of pirates as humane captors. It focuses on the traumatic experiences of kidnapped crew members, who are often told by shipping companies not to speak publicly about their ordeals because this will deter people from wanting to work on ships. The report describes as 'staggering' the human toll on captured crew, the majority of whom come from places like the Philippines, India and Bangladesh, and, unlike Western hostages, do not capture the attention of the international media:

> Both successful and unsuccessful attacks expose seafarers
> to dangerous experiences, with the potential for long-term

physical and psychological trauma. Somali pirates are heavily armed, frequently with automatic weapons, rocket-propelled grenades, and explosives. Pirates attack ships, abuse seafarers, and place hostages in the complete control of heavily armed men, all of which have the potential to cause serious injury or even death to seafarers. Additionally, the long-term psychological impact of these experiences, though subtler and more difficult to detect, is nevertheless severe.[23]

The report said that in 2010 alone, more than four thousand seafarers were attacked with firearms, and others used as human shields. It said the average time in captivity was five months. It also described different forms of torture:

shooting at hostages with water cannons, locking hostages in the ship's freezer, tying hostages up on deck exposed to scorching sun, and hanging hostages by their feet submerged in the sea ... hanging them from the mast and meat hooks ... parading hostages naked around the vessel ... and subjecting them to mock executions.[24]

It quotes one man, an engine technician, who was held hostage on the MV *Marida Marguerite*: 'They took me on deck one day and tied my hands and my legs behind my back for two hours, and also tightened a cable around my genitals ... When I screamed, they tightened it more.'[25] An Indian former hostage, Dipendra Rathore, whose ship was seized in April 2010, said he was still traumatized by the experience:

They kept us in a state of terror – we were beaten constantly with metal poles ... I saw my crewmates being thrashed with sticks and having electric probes attached to their genitals, and one man was suspended by ropes from the ship's mast for several hours. Even when I could not see the torturing, I could hear the screams. I can still hear the screams to this day.[26]

In light of these experiences, the advice offered in the European Union naval force's guide *Surviving Piracy off the Coast of Somalia* seems somewhat limited: 'If your vessel has been pirated, accept that you may be held in captivity for an extended period of time. Typically periods of detention range from six to twelve weeks, but may last considerably longer depending on the success of the negotiations.'[27]

As the transitional government of Somalia does not control the areas of the country affected by piracy, it is unable to take effective action to deal with the problem. In October 2009, the then prime minister of Somalia, Omar Sharmarke, assured me his government would eliminate piracy off the coast of Somalia within the next two years. He brushed off my suggestion that this might be something of a challenge given that the authority of his government was restricted to a few streets of the capital, Mogadishu: 'We are not powerless, but our capacity to handle this issue is not all there. That is why we are seeking assistance and investment from overseas. We will eradicate piracy through a civil affairs and information campaign, backed by military force.'

As previously mentioned, the Union of Islamic Courts managed to dramatically reduce the problem of piracy. Hansen describes how the authorities in the self-declared republic of Somaliland have also had some success in combating piracy:

> Somaliland's achievements in the struggle against piracy are amazing ... Despite having a very weak coastguard service, pirate attacks in their part of the Somali maritime economic zone number less than one every two years over the last ten years. Somaliland reacts fast against rumoured pirate groups, catching pirates when they are in the process of organising themselves.[28]

It is interesting that the Union of Islamic Courts and the authorities in Somaliland have been more successful at reducing piracy than the hugely expensive international naval patrols off the coast of Somalia, which have included not just joint operations, such as the EU and NATO task forces, but warships from single countries, including Russia, Iran, India, China and Japan. This is proof perhaps that the problem can best be tackled on land, with largely home-grown Somali solutions, possibly supported by some form of foreign assistance.

Piracy has led to a distorted world-view of Somalia. The dominant image is of a drought-ridden country, occupied by al-Qaeda-linked insurgents, surrounded by pirate-infested waters. It cannot be denied that a relatively small number of pirates have caused large-scale havoc. But the fact that effective solutions have been found by small, local and relatively weak authority structures suggests that a different approach could be explored, learning from the examples of the UIC and Somaliland.

6 | SOMALIA AND THE OUTSIDE WORLD

Foreign interventions in Somalia since the fall of Siad Barre in 1991 have largely failed to achieve their aims, as have most other attempts by outsiders to help rebuild the state or otherwise resolve the country's problems. Some have had virtually no impact. Others have made things worse. In spite of all the interventions, as Lindley points out, Somalis have not allowed themselves to become mere pawns of foreigners:

> Outside interventions have often played a significant role in laying the groundwork for conflict and state collapse. In Somalia, Cold War military sponsorship (and its switching and withdrawal), international aid (and its gluts and stoppages), and neo-liberal reforms (and their misconceptions) helped to destabilise the state, and international intervention has conspicuously failed to resolve the conflict in the two decades since it began. But beyond the failed blueprints for change, life in the Somali region goes on, witness to various forms of social, economic and political innovation and change.[1]

Those in power do not agree that their policies towards Somalia have failed. The British former prime minister, Tony Blair, was asked in September 2010 whether he thought the Western approach towards Somalia and Yemen had backfired, strengthening rather than weakening al-Qaeda and other extremist groups:

> When these groups in Yemen and Somalia kill innocent people, it is not us who have provoked them to do it. We have got to

stop them. It's rubbish to say we are provoking them to do it ... I do not agree that Western policies have made these groups stronger in Yemen and in Somalia. Western policies are designed to confront what is wrong, regressive, wicked and backward looking.[2]

Somalia has been a major headache for foreign powers during many periods of its history. As far back as the early 1900s, the dervish forces of the 'Mad Mullah' disrupted colonial ambitions, especially those of the British. The interventions by the United States and United Nations in the early 1990s were especially traumatic; what was initially supposed to be a humanitarian mission ended up with US and UN forces becoming an integral part of the conflict, viewed as an enemy by many of the people they had originally intended to help. It was here that the term 'mission creep' was first used to describe how a foreign intervention can end up trying to achieve something entirely different and more complicated than what it first set out to do.[3]

The UN secretary-general at the time of these disastrous foreign interventions was Boutros Boutros-Ghali. In 1996, he described how Somalia represented one of the most difficult challenges ever faced by the United Nations: 'The efforts of the United Nations to end the human suffering in Somalia, foster reconciliation among the warring factions and promote national reconciliation led to one of the most challenging, arduous undertakings in the organization's fifty-year history.'

After the humiliating and expensive failure of the UN and US missions, foreign powers and international institutions largely withdrew from Somalia. Some parts of the country settled into an almost permanent state of insecurity, fragmenting into a patchwork of continuously shifting power blocs, often at war with each other. Other parts of the territory went their own way, the most extreme example being Somaliland in the north-west, which declared itself independent and, with virtually no outside help, built itself into a functioning political and economic entity.

Bringing peace and lasting stability to Somalia represents a huge and as yet unresolved challenge for foreign policy-makers. It is much easier to say what does not work for Somalia than what does. Large-scale military interventions have failed. Keeping Somalia at arm's length by holding peace conferences on foreign soil has also failed. There is no guarantee that trying to emulate the relative success stories of Somaliland and, to a lesser extent, Puntland and other semi-autonomous regions would work, as following this formula would, in all probability, lead to the fragmentation of Somalia as a nation-state.

Somalia and the 'War on Terror'

The growth of Islamist violence in the region and elsewhere in the world brought Somalia back on to the international radar. Key events were the 1998 bombings of the US embassies in Kenya and Tanzania, and the world-changing al-Qaeda attacks on the United States on 11 September 2001. The Somali Islamist movement al-Itihaad was put on the US list of terrorist-related organizations, as was the Somali money transfer company al-Barakat. Two months after the 9/11 attacks, the American authorities ordered the closure of al-Barakat. They accused the Somali owner of the company, Ahmed Ali Jimale, of being a friend and supporter of Osama bin Laden, managing his finances, and transferring al-Qaeda money to wherever in the world it was required. As previously mentioned, the company's bank accounts were frozen, meaning Somalis in the diaspora could not send money home to relatives who depended on remittances for their survival. President George W. Bush made generous use of 'War on Terror' rhetoric when, in November 2001, he announced the closure of al-Barakat:

> By shutting these networks down, we disrupt the murderers' work. Today's action interrupts Al Qaeda's communications; it

blocks an important source of funds. It provides us with valuable information and sends a clear message to global financial institutions; you are with us or you are with the terrorists. And if you're with the terrorists, you will face the consequences. We fight an enemy who hides in caves in Afghanistan, and in the shadows within our own society. It's an enemy who can only survive in darkness. Today, we've taken another important action to expose the enemy to the light and disrupt its ability to threaten American and innocent life.[4]

Less than a year later, al-Barakat was taken off the US terror list as insufficient evidence could be found to prove that it was a conduit for al-Qaeda finances. But it was too late; the USA had alienated many in Somalia by severing a lifeline for hundreds of thousands of people, and by so closely associating al-Itihaad and al-Barakat with al-Qaeda. By linking these organizations with terrorism, the USA contributed to a new way of thinking about Somalia; events in the country were increasingly seen through the prism of al-Qaeda and violent Islamism. History was rewritten by some who said al-Qaeda was responsible for the killing in 1993 of the eighteen US servicemen in Mogadishu. The events of 9/11 and the subsequent 'War on Terror' shaped the way the USA and others approached Somalia; in many ways it became a testing ground for the way global powers dealt with militant Islamism, especially its presence in Africa.

The Bush administration's National Security Strategy of 2002 reflected the new post-9/11 approach towards Africa, which focused largely on counter-terrorism efforts: 'In Africa, promise and opportunity sit side by side with disease, war and desperate poverty. This threatens both a core value of the United States – preserving human dignity – and our strategic priority – combating global terror.'[5] Four years later, US strategy went farther. Africa was identified as 'a high priority'. The 2006 National Security

Strategy document stated that 'our security depends upon partnering with Africans to strengthen fragile and failing states and bring ungoverned areas under the control of effective democracies'.[6]

The rise to power of the Union of Islamic Courts (UIC) marked another turning point in foreign policy towards Somalia. The USA and others seemed incapable of perceiving what was initially a loose alliance of highly localized sharia courts as anything other than an al-Qaeda-linked threat. Local and foreign adversaries of the UIC, especially Somali warlords and Ethiopia, used and manipulated to their own advantage America's concerns about the movement. The warlords, who felt threatened by the growing power and popularity of the courts, fed into Washington's fears of a growing Islamist threat in Somalia by presenting the UIC as a breeding ground for radicalism and a potential haven for jihadi elements. The USA bought into this idea, supporting the formation by the warlords of the Alliance for the Restoration of Peace and Counter-Terrorism. The use of the words 'peace' and 'counter-terrorism' in the Alliance's title was a cynical move on behalf of the warlords, possibly designed to win the support of the USA; the warlords themselves were far more interested in regaining the power they had lost to the UIC than in fighting 'terrorism' and restoring peace.

In a sense, the USA and its allies decided Somalia was a new front for al-Qaeda a few years before it became one in reality. This approach may well have contributed to the growth of radical Islamism in Somalia; treating Somalis as if they were terrorists may have pushed some in the country towards militancy. Labelling Somalia in this way also served to inadvertently advertise it as an attractive destination for foreign jihadis keen to globalize their activities, and to find a foothold in sub-Saharan Africa. As the anthropologist Markus Virgil Hoehne writes, research suggests that Washington may have been wrong to be so quick in identifying Somalia as a haven for Islamist terrorists:

Contrary to the assumption about 'black holes' and ungoverned spaces voiced by politicians and some academics,
the Harmony Project of the Center for Combating Terrorism at West Point has recently shown that the absence of
a government in Somalia did not automatically provide
fertile ground for Al Qaeda terrorism. Its researchers, who
had access to declassified intelligence reports on Al Qaeda
activities in the Horn in the early 1990s concluded that the
foreign Islamist activists faced similar problems as did the UN
and US humanitarian and military intervention in Somalia
(1992–1995): they were partly distrusted as 'foreigners' who
adhered to a version of Islam that was not popular in Somalia,
they ran into problems with always changing clan and sub-clan
alliances, they suffered from the weak infrastructure of the
country, they lacked security, they were exposed to external
interventions since no government could uphold Somalia's
sovereignty, and they were at risk of being 'sold' by petty
criminals and others in Somalia to the enemy (the US).[7]

The Ethiopian invasion

Anxious to avoid a repetition of the disastrous intervention
of the early 1990s, the USA was keen not to engage in direct
large-scale military action against what it perceived as the al-
Qaeda threat emanating from Somalia. It found a convenient ally
in Ethiopia, which it promoted as a key partner in the 'War on
Terror', and was itself opposed to the Union of Islamic Courts.
Although a willing partner, Ethiopia was a particularly poor choice
owing to its long history of enmity with Somalia; any Ethiopian
involvement would be seen as highly provocative by the majority
of the Somali population.

With US backing, Ethiopia launched a full-scale invasion
in December 2006, sending in 14,000 troops and carrying out
aerial bombardments of strategic locations in Mogadishu. At the

same time, the USA carried out a number of air strikes against senior al-Qaeda and other Islamist suspects it said were hiding in Somalia. Most of these attacks did not hit their intended targets, if indeed they were in Somalia at the time, killing civilians instead, including nomads and their livestock. This action further alienated the population, and may well have provoked more Somalis into joining radical and violent religious groups.

The US Assistant Secretary of State for African Affairs at the time, Jendayi Frazer, was instrumental in designing this policy, one of the most counterproductive foreign initiatives towards Somalia in recent years. She stated that the UIC was closely linked with Islamist radicals, alleging that al-Qaeda had sidelined the moderates in the movement and taken over its leadership. She said the courts received funding from Eritrea, Yemen, Egypt and Saudi Arabia, accusing Eritrea of breaking the international arms embargo against Somalia by sending weapons to the UIC. At times Ms Frazer appeared to be trying to micro-manage the situation in Somalia. She made repeated detailed statements about every twist and turn, calling on moderates to join the reconciliation process and to distance themselves from those she described as extremists.

Ms Frazer came to personify the Western approach to Somalia, and was as a result verbally attacked by leading Islamist figures. In 2009 an audio message purporting to be from Osama bin Laden in which he called for the ousting of the newly elected president, Sheikh Sharif Sheikh Ahmed, whom he described as a tool of the United States, was posted on the Internet. Bin Laden said the election of Sheikh Sharif was a result of what he described as the 'temptations and offers' from 'that American woman'.

The Ethiopian invasion succeeded in driving the UIC from power but, instead of eliminating Islamist extremism, it led to the development of groups far more radical than the courts' union. The main one was the courts' militia, al-Shabaab, led by the

Afghan-trained Adan Hashi Ayro. Instead of fleeing to Eritrea like many UIC elements, it melted away into the bush near the border with Kenya, only to re-emerge as a ferocious fighting force. Al-Shabaab eventually took over most of southern and central Somalia, including large parts of Mogadishu.

Parallels can be drawn with the Islamic Salvation Front (FIS) in Algeria, which was prevented by the military from taking power after elections in 1991. Efforts to eliminate the FIS backfired, and instead it transformed itself into something far more radical. A decade-long Islamist insurgency followed in which tens of thousands of people were killed, many by having their throats slit. This later led to the emergence of the al-Qaeda branch in North Africa, al-Qaeda in the Islamic Maghreb.

The Ethiopian invasion and resulting conflict in Mogadishu led to one of the worst humanitarian crises ever experienced in Somalia. Between 2007 and 2008, about two-thirds of the city's population fled, many to ramshackle camps on the outskirts of Mogadishu, where it was often too dangerous for humanitarian supplies to be delivered. Others left for already overburdened refugee camps in Kenya, Djibouti, Yemen, Somaliland and Puntland. Parts of Mogadishu were almost entirely emptied of their civilian populations, being transformed into urban battlegrounds for the Ethiopian forces, transitional government troops, clan militias and Islamist fighters. In a paper for the US-based Foreign Policy Institute, Bronwyn Bruton describes how the Ethiopian invasion led to a surge in Islamist activities:

> The presence of the TFG [transitional federal government] and especially of Ethiopian troops sparked a complex insurgency in Mogadishu. The Shabaab militia started to gain popular backing as a resistance movement. Foreign jihadists, including Al Qaeda, sensed an unprecedented opportunity to globalize Somalia's conflict and quickly funnelled support to

the Shabaab. Several dozen foreign jihadists entered Somalia, importing Al Qaeda tactics. Remote-controlled detonations and suicide bombings became relatively common, and over the course of two years, the Shabaab captured most of southern Somalia.[8]

The mission backfires

It could be argued that it would have been more productive for foreign powers to engage with the Union of Islamic Courts instead of trying to destroy it. It had after all brought a degree of stability and order to people's lives for the brief six months it was in power. There were moderate as well as radical elements within the movement. It was by no means a foregone conclusion that US fears about the UIC would have been realized if it had been allowed to remain in power and further consolidate its position. According to the Somali academic Professor Abdi Samatar, the UIC 'was ready and willing to engage with the United States'[9] but was unable to do so owing to the hostility of Ms Frazer and other US officials.

It is ironic that Sheikh Sharif Sheikh Ahmed, who was in 2009 elected president of Somalia's internationally backed transitional federal government, was a former leader of the UIC. If the foreign community is prepared to work with him in this incarnation, why was it not prepared to do so when he led the UIC? It is possible the courts' union would have pursued a relatively moderate approach if it had been assured of the support of the United Nations, the United States and other powers. But Sheikh Sharif Sheikh Ahmed is now seen as a sell-out, his authority rejected by many Somalis, who regard him as a Western proxy.

As Bruton argues, it is difficult to understand why the series of transitional administrations have continued to be internationally recognized as the legitimate authority in Somalia:

The current policy of providing military and diplomatic

support for the TFG is not bearing fruit. It is also extremely costly. The military stalemate that has held since May 7, 2009, has displaced more than two hundred thousand people from Mogadishu – prolonging a cycle of suffering and radicalization and adding to an already horrendous refugee problem on the Kenyan border. That is a terribly high price to pay for protecting a government that commands little support on the ground, administers no territory, and has, despite the efforts of the international community over the past five years, developed no institutional or military capacity to govern the country. Without supportive political momentum on the ground, the current peacekeeping mission is likely to be as futile as the Ethiopian invasion, and may end in the same way, with an embarrassing withdrawal of troops.[10]

A 2010 report for the UN Security Council was especially damning about the transitional government's security apparatus: 'Despite infusions of foreign training and assistance, government security forces remain ineffective, disorganized and corrupt – a composite of independent militias loyal to senior government officials and military officers who profit from the business of war and resist their integration under a single command.'[11]

Some of the problems faced by Somali government troops were revealed in a US diplomatic cable released by the whistle-blowing website Wikileaks, which describes a 'brief Nairobi airport meeting' between an American diplomat and the former prime minister of Somalia, Omar Abdirashid Ali Sharmarke.[12] A major topic of conversation was radios – or the lack of them. Mr Sharmarke explains to the diplomat how a shortage of this most basic form of military equipment led to the failure of a major counter-attack against al-Shabaab by government troops and African Union peacekeepers in Mogadishu. The troops could speak to each other only by mobile phone, which led to serious misunderstandings;

AU troops beat a hasty retreat because they had received unclear information, believing, wrongly, that they had been cut off by the insurgents. The cable describes how Mr Sharmarke begged the diplomat for walkie-talkies and other forms of battlefield communication.

For a significant period, the Somali government could not even operate from Mogadishu because of the insecurity and the hostility of the city's population. When it returned to the capital from the regional town of Baidoa, it depended for its survival first on the Ethiopian forces and later on the presence of Ugandan and Burundian peacekeeping troops. Members of parliament and other officials spend much of their time living in hotels in Kenya and elsewhere because Mogadishu remains such a difficult and hostile environment. The British former minister for Africa, Chris Mullin, writes in his diaries about a Nairobi meeting he had in 2004 with the president of Somalia's transitional government, Abdullahi Yusuf: 'Item One on today's long agenda: a call on Abdullahi Yusuf, the new "President" of Somalia. At the moment, of course, he is nothing of the sort. Just a man in a hotel in Nairobi. Later, in another hotel, I addressed the new Somali "parliament", which comprises some of the very people who have reduced Somalia to rubble.'[13]

A Somali former foreign minister, Ismail Mohamed Huure, or Booba, described the life of Somalia's semi-exiled politicians when I met him in his rooms in the Andalus Hotel in Nairobi:

Nairobi is more or less the central meeting place for Somalis. Anyone who wants to keep in touch with what is happening in Somali has to be either in Somalia or in Nairobi, possibly even in this hotel, because almost every day someone arrives from Somalia bringing with them all the latest news.

In some ways I consider this hotel to be my home. When you are in a hotel like this, a Somali hotel, where at least ninety per cent of the residents are Somali, you don't feel that you are too far away from home. The discussions we have in this hotel used to take place in the teashops of Mogadishu. I definitely feel this is home; I have been living like this, in hotels in Kenya, for about ten years. In some ways it is very sad for me and the other Somali politicians living here in Kenya. We feel at home but we are not at home. The news coming from Somalia is usually terrible so we often feel overwhelmed with stress.

The fact that the transitional government was able to return to Mogadishu only as a result of a US-backed military intervention by Ethiopia meant many Somalis considered it an illegitimate foreign implant. The transitional federal government is known by the derogatory Somali nickname *daba dhilif*, which translates roughly as a 'government set up for a foreign purpose' or a 'satellite government'. The USA, the UN and others failed to recognize that, for a government to be considered legitimate by Somalis, it cannot be associated with foreigners.

The supply by the USA of weapons to the Somali government – such as in May and June 2009, when it provided 94 tonnes of arms and ammunition[14] – and the training by foreign security experts of transitional government forces provide ammunition for those opposing the central administration in the country. They can describe it as a foreign puppet, its existence dependent on the support and protection of outsiders.

There has been some disagreement within the US administration about how best to approach the problem of Somalia. Some, such as the State Department's most senior official for Africa, Johnnie Carson, appear keen to avoid an on-the-ground US presence, fearing that such a policy would lead to increased support for al-Shabaab and other anti-Western groups. As Carson put it, 'we do not want an American footprint or boot on the ground' in Somalia.

However, US military and intelligence agencies have stepped up operations inside Somalia, sometimes through indirect means. In 2011, the Pentagon approved US$45 million in arms shipments to African Union peacekeepers in Mogadishu. The *New York Times* reported in August 2011 that French, South African and Scandinavian former soldiers working for the US-based private security firm Bancroft Global Development ran a fortified camp in Mogadishu, training African troops in the art of urban warfare. The paper also reports that the CIA has helped build a large base at Mogadishu airport, referred to by Somalis as 'the Pink House' owing to the colour of the buildings, or simply 'Guantánamo'. The *New York Times* says CIA operatives have carried out joint interrogations of suspected terrorists in a Somali prison, and have covertly trained intelligence operatives:

> Unlike regular Somali government troops, the CIA-trained Somali commandos are outfitted with new weapons and flak jackets, and are given sunglasses and ski masks to conceal their identities. They are part of the Somali National Security Agency – an intelligence organization financed largely by the CIA – which answers to Somalia's Transitional Federal Government. Many in Mogadishu, though, believe that the Somali intelligence service is building a power base independent of the weak government.[15]

It has been suggested that the improved fighting skills of AU and Somali troops, largely a result of direct and indirect US assistance, led to the retreat of many al-Shabaab fighters from Mogadishu in 2011. It is unclear whether the Islamist insurgency has been permanently weakened, or has simply entered another stage, whereby it will pursue hit-and-run terror tactics. The recent history of US involvement in Somalia, which has been described as 'a graveyard for American missions', suggests the less visible the involvement the better. Anything seen as remotely 'American' could provide fertile propaganda material for Islamist groups, and provoke hostility from many other Somalis.

Although the US insisted it was completely taken by surprise by Kenya's invasion of Somalia in October 2011, it shares Kenya's interest in defeating al-Shabaab and is a long-standing security partner of Kenya. The increase in US drone attacks at the time of Kenya's military action led many in Somalia to interpret the invasion as a US project. In some parts of Somalia, especially where civilians were killed by the 'invaders', this led to increased hatred of the US and growing sympathy for al-Shabaab. The Kenyan intervention also seriously disrupted humanitarian efforts during a period of famine.

Those interested in state-building and improving security in Somalia might do better by studying those political experiments which have worked in the country, the two most obvious being those of Somaliland and the Union of Islamic Courts. Both of these developed from the 'bottom up', and fused traditional Somali ways of life with more modern methods. The USA and Britain have recognized this belatedly; in 2010 the USA announced a dual-track policy towards Somalia, continuing to recognize and support the government in Mogadishu, but increasing its engagement with and support for the more stable regions in the north, especially Somaliland and Puntland. Britain has also started to engage more actively with these two regions; a confidential US cable from 2009 describes how 'the UK plans "to thicken" its support to Somaliland, though the British government is not considering recognition at this stage'.[16] President Obama has at the same time continued to pursue the previous US administration's policy of treating Somalia as a terrorist threat. He made this clear when he visited Africa in 2009: 'When there is genocide in Darfur or terrorism in Somalia, these are not simply African problems, they are global security challenges, and they demand a global response.'

The end results of the Ethiopian invasion of Somalia were not only the installation of a weak and unpopular government in Mogadishu, the displacement of hundreds of thousands of people, and a significant increase in violence, but also the radicalization of a small group of dedicated jihadists. They formed the core of the Islamist fighting force al-Shabaab, which within a few years would control most of southern and central Somalia, forcing a way of life on people that they have never known before or ever wanted to experience. Virgil Hoehne describes how US Ethiopian policy in many ways created the monster it was trying to destroy:

> In 2009, after three years of insurgency and fighting, the militant Somali Islamists, particularly Al Shabaab, in fact resemble the battle-hardened and ideologically uncompromising Taliban of 1996, ready to rule a country. In this sense, the anti-Islamist propaganda of 2006 has fulfilled itself. Somalia since 2006 is possibly the clearest example for the failure of US (and Ethiopian) counter-terrorism policy, which actually has produced what it was supposed to counter.[17]

The Islamists take hold

The Ethiopians officially withdrew from Somalia in January 2009 but maintained a military presence in the country, especially in the border regions. Ethiopia has provided support to groups opposed to the Islamists, such as the Sufi movement Ahlu Sunna Wa Jamaa, which has been in uneasy alliance with the transitional government and fights against al-Shabaab in southern and central Somalia. The USA has continued to attack Somalia from the sky, carrying out targeted bombings from military aircraft and unmanned drones. In May 2008 the al-Shabaab leader, Adan Hashi Ayro, was killed in such an attack. A US diplomatic cable entitled 'Ayro's demise' predicted that his death would have 'several positive impacts', including the short-term disruption of al-Shabaab attacks, a leadership struggle within the movement, and improved prospects for Somali reconciliation. However, the often fractured movement was, if anything, strengthened by the killing of Ayro. Its members united in their anger, which spurred them on to fight against what they saw as the 'infidel' transitional government and any other groups sponsored by foreign powers. The Somalilander Ahmed Abdi Godane, who was at least as radical as Ayro, was appointed as the new leader of the movement.

Just as President Bush used 'War on Terror' language to announce the closure of a Somali remittance company, al-Shabaab uses typical jihadi rhetoric to threaten the United States. In January 2010, its spokesman, Sheikh Ali Mohamud Raaghe, issued a warning to the newly elected president, Barack Obama:

> If Obama were to send his army to Somalia, his men would suffer the same fate as in 1993 when they were dragged through the streets of Mogadishu and their planes littered the streets of the city. If the US wants to send its army to Somalia we will teach them a lesson. I promise we will fight them even harder than we fight against those African forces who are here right now. My message to Obama is, do not send the American boys here, and do not spend your wealth on a battle you will never win.

The challenge of aid

The Islamist insurgency in Somalia represents more than a foreign policy challenge. It has also become a domestic problem for countries hosting Somali refugees, including Kenya, Yemen, the United States, Britain, Australia and Scandinavia, where disaffected young Somalis either return home to join the jihad, or plot terrorist attacks in their host countries. This growing internationalization of the Somali insurgency, together with the presence of non-Somali fighters in al-Shabaab, means that it has become a truly global problem.

9 An al-Shabaab fighter distributes food parcels in Lower Shabelle famine zone, September 2011 (al-Shabaab)

Apart from the existence of the Islamist insurgency in Somalia, and the threat it poses to the outside world, the ongoing humanitarian crisis in the country also represents a significant challenge for foreign powers. Aid agencies have faced immense difficulty delivering emergency supplies to those who need them most; humanitarian workers have been killed and kidnapped, militias demand extortionate fees at roadblocks, and al-Shabaab has at times forbidden aid agencies from working in the areas it controls. This became a particular problem in July 2011 when the UN declared a famine in two regions controlled by al-Shabaab, Bakol and Lower Shabelle. By treading very carefully, the UN and other agencies made some progress in discussions with al-Shabaab about bringing aid into these areas. The USA then announced that it too would channel humanitarian supplies to al-Shabaab territory, as long as the UN could guarantee security. Shortly after the US announcement, al-Shabaab declared that it would not allow foreign agencies in, possibly provoked by the rather brash, unsubtle American approach. Once again, the USA misjudged the situation in Somalia, disrupting the patient and painstaking approach of other humanitarian groups which had managed to continue working in al-Shabaab areas throughout the aid ban.

According to the United Nations, another problem has been corruption at the very heart of the aid delivery system. A UN Security Council report found in 2010 that up to half the food aid intended for some two and a half million Somalis was being diverted to corrupt contractors, Islamist groups and humanitarian workers. The report said the UN World Food Programme (WFP) had awarded 80 per cent of the contracts for the transportation of food aid, worth US$200 million, to just three Somali business-men, who sold the food illegally, for their own profit. The report said some of the aid had been used to fuel the conflict: 'Some humanitarian resources, notably food aid, have been diverted to military uses. A handful of Somali contractors for aid agencies have formed a cartel and become important power brokers – some of whom channel their profits – or the aid itself – directly to armed opposition groups.'[18] The WFP denied the allegations but said it would stop using the three transporters pending investigations.

It is not only powerful Somali businessmen who take advantage of aid organizations. With their years of experience in receiving foreign aid, many others in Somalia have become experts at exploiting humanitarian groups. I witnessed this in Somaliland in 1994 as representatives from UN agencies and other humanitarian groups rushed in to help people during a period of inter-clan conflict. I travelled with a crisis team of foreign aid experts to the town of Odweyne. The first thing we did was meet the mayor, who read out a detailed list of what was 'urgently required' by the people he said had fled to his town from fighting elsewhere in the territory. 'In total, we have 6,100 beneficiaries, many of whom are starving, malnourished and without shelter. Five hundred people have already died from war wounds, hunger and disease. We need plastic sheeting, blankets, clothes, beans, oil, cooking pots and medicine.'

As I walked around Odweyne, it soon became obvious that there were nowhere near 6,100 'beneficiaries'. There were perhaps a few dozen. None of them was starving, disease-ridden or homeless as they had all been taken in by local families. The aid agencies did little to correct the picture; a humanitarian disaster in Somaliland meant more contracts and more funding – it kept them in business.

Regional implications

The crisis in Somalia has affected many countries in East Africa and the Horn. Refugees have poured across borders. Violence has destabilized neighbouring countries, dragging some directly into the conflict, either as peacekeepers, or to protect or advance their own interests. What was initially a local form of militant Islam has developed into a regional, even international, force. An indication of how countries in the region are concerned about the situation in Somalia is that some of them, including Uganda, Kenya, Ethiopia and Djibouti, have allowed Somali troops to be trained on their territory, sometimes with the help of Western security experts. Uganda and Burundi have provided peacekeeping troops, and regional groups, such as IGAD and the African Union, have had endless conferences on the situation in Somalia. These have had as little positive impact as those organized by the UN, the European Union and other bodies.

Burundi and Uganda are affected not only because they provide troops for the peacekeeping operation, dozens of whom have lost their lives, but because they face retaliatory action from al-Shabaab and other opposition groups as a result of having forces on the ground in Somalia. In July 2010, al-Shabaab carried

10 Displaced people queue for food rations in Mogadishu (Mohamed Moalimuu)

out twin bomb attacks in the Ugandan capital, Kampala, killing more than seventy people.

Despite their relative stability, the Somali regions of Puntland and Somaliland are not immune from Islamist attacks. In October 2008, triple suicide bombings in Hargeisa left many dead. Puntland was attacked on the same day, an indication of al-Shabaab's ability to carry out sophisticated, coordinated attacks.

Ethiopia and Eritrea

Ethiopia, in particular, cannot be disentangled from the conflict in Somalia. The two countries have for decades been uncomfortable neighbours, with full-scale hostilities periodically breaking out. A major reason for this perpetual state of unease is Ethiopia's 'Somali Region', which has a long border with Somalia, and is affected by a long-running internal rebellion. Ethiopia maintains what is in effect an informal buffer zone with Somalia. The presence in Somalia of Ethiopian troops is reported so frequently that it has ceased to become 'news'. As Ethiopia is now a key Western partner in the 'War on Terror', its involvement in Somalia has acquired a global dimension, as it did during the Cold War in the 1970s.

Another country deeply involved in Somalia is Eritrea. Its engagement has to be understood in terms of its continuing dispute with Ethiopia, against which it fought a bitter war from 1998 to 2000, a few years after it became independent from Addis Ababa. Eritrea sees Somalia's transitional federal government as an Ethiopian proxy, and therefore supports groups that oppose it. The UN, the USA and others have consistently accused Eritrea of providing political, financial, diplomatic and military support to Islamist groups, in violation of an international arms embargo against Somalia. It has also been accused of providing training facilities for Somali Islamist groups in Assab in eastern Eritrea and Teseney in the west.[19] It was to Asmara that leaders of the UIC fled following the Ethiopian invasion of Somalia in 2006, setting up a government in exile to rival the internationally recognized transitional federal government in Somalia.

A leaked cable from the American embassy in Asmara describes how, shortly after Barack Obama took office, Eritrea embarked on a charm offensive towards the USA. As part of the initiative, the American ambassador and his wife were invited to spend a day with senior officials on a farm belonging to Eritrea's economic director, described in the cable as 'the architect of the country's imploding economy'. The rest of the cable had an equally sarcastic tone: 'Lunch was served in a rocky gulch beneath a thorny acacia tree. The ambassador and his wife were treated with grilled sheep innards served with honey and a chili sauce, but no silverware, washed down with a sour, semi-fermented drink called, aptly, "*sewa*".'[20]

The lunch did not appear to help much; the cable goes on to describe America's deep concern about Eritrea's relationship with al-Shabaab, reporting how one Eritrean official acknowledged limited contact with the movement. It adds that the USA issued a blunt warning to Eritrea of serious consequences if it continued to support al-Shabaab.

Eritrea has been equally critical of the USA. In August 2007, the Eritrean president, Isaias Afewerki, accused America of trying to harm his country's interests, calling on Washington to end what he described as acts of adventurism. He warned that US foreign policy was leading the world on what he called a dangerous path. Shortly before Afewerki's statement, the US Assistant Secretary of State for African Affairs, Jendayi Frazer, had said America was considering putting Eritrea on the list of state sponsors of terrorism.

Somali Islamists do not deny that they have received support from Eritrea. In 2011 the Islamist leader Hassin Dahir Aweys openly acknowledged Eritrean involvement:

> We are very grateful to Eritrea for two reasons. It refused to support the aggression against us and it welcomed our people. Also, it gave us political support. Eritrea is a very poor country, and it has been punished because of its small show of sympathy towards us. Anyone who as much as smiles at us is punished very harshly. Now Eritrea is in a very difficult situation. We are sad because Eritrea has been punished because of us ... The United Nations is blaming Eritrea just because it helped people who have been wronged. Now Eritrea itself is being condemned. To condemn people who help poor people who have been wronged, who have been invaded, is mind-boggling.

Yemen

Yemen has also been affected by the conflict in Somalia. It hosts many Somali refugees, dozens of whom die every year when boats transporting them capsize in the Gulf of Aden. Islamist insurgents in the two countries have become involved in each other's campaigns, with al-Shabaab sending fighters to Yemen, and Yemeni jihadis fighting in Somalia. This was acknowledged in 2010 by al-Shabaab's spokesman, Sheikh Ali Mohamud Raaghe: 'On the issue of Yemen, the forces we are sending them and the fighters they are sending us has something to do with the close relationship between both sides. That is all I am going to say about the matter as we have decided not to discuss it in the media.'

Shortly after this, the deputy leader of al-Qaeda in the Arabian Peninsula, Saeed al Shihri, praised al-Shabaab in an audio record-ing posted on the Internet:

> I say to our great brothers in Somalia; may God bless you with the best reward and thank you for sending your forces to us ... Despite the difficulties and harassments you are experiencing in your own jihad, you have still offered to send forces to support us ... Each from his front, we shall cooperate in our upcoming battle with the United States, which is the head of global infidelity.

Kenya

Another country deeply affected by the conflict in Somalia is Kenya. Tens of thousands of Somalis have flooded into the country in the past few years, especially as the conflict intensified in southern Somalia. Matters were made even worse by severe drought and famine in 2011. Dadaab refugee camp in northern Kenya, which hosts mainly Somali refugees, is the largest refugee camp in the world. It cannot cope with the continuing influx of people. Originally meant to host 90,000 people, by November 2011 it had nearly 500,000 residents, living in cramped, over-crowded conditions, and subject to brutal harassment by the Kenyan security forces.[21] According to the UN, about 200,000 people arrived in Dadaab in 2011 alone.

The troublesome relationship between Kenya and Somalia stretches back for decades. Even before independence in 1960, Somalia was keen to include as part of its territory the Northern Frontier District of colonial Kenya. This region bordered southern Somalia and was populated by a predominantly ethnic Somali population. After prolonged negotiations, Britain decided it should remain part of Kenya, prompting Somalia to sever diplomatic relations with the UK. Given the continuous difficulties it has with this region, Kenya may in some ways regret that it did not cede this parched stretch of land to Somalia.

North-eastern Kenya has been especially tense in recent years following the occupation by al-Shabaab of much of the adjoining Somali territory. Kenyan frontier guards are stationed almost within spitting distance of Islamist militiamen. Even though the border is officially closed, it is impossible to control because it is so long and porous. Kenyan Somalis in the region complain that young men in their communities are recruited by al-Shabaab and taken across the border to fight. The USA says it has 'reason to believe that some limited recruitment by *Al Shabaab* has occurred in Dadaab refugee camp'.[22]

Sometimes the conflict in Somalia spills over into Kenya. In October 2010, fighting broke out between a clan militia and al-Shabaab in the frontier town of Belet Hawa. Hundreds of people fled across the border into the Kenyan town of Mandera, which is only about three kilometres away from Belet Hawa.

With conflict so close by, Kenya has made it a priority to protect itself, and has taken part in a regional programme to train Somali soldiers and police. There have been reports that some of the 2,500 recruits are not Somali nationals, but Kenyans of Somali ethnicity. Kenya has been an active supporter of the 'Jubaland offensive', a plan to take back from al-Shabaab the southernmost parts of Somalia, and to set up some kind of buffer zone between the two countries. The authorities in Kenya took things a significant step further in October 2011 when, following the abduction by Somalis of four foreign nationals from its territory, it sent hundreds of troops deep into Somalia. Kenya blamed al-Shabaab for the kidnappings, and said it would continue its air and ground assault against the group until Kenya was safe from what it described as 'the al-Shabaab menace'. Al-Shabaab denied any role in the kidnappings, and said Kenya's inexperienced military would 'taste the pain of mujahideen bullets'.

Kenya is caught in a difficult position. It cannot afford to ignore the Somali problem, but by invading Somali territory it has not only invited increased hostility from al-Shabaab, but from many other Somalis too. Its cooperation with the United States and Europe in their 'War on Terror', and the presence in the port city of Mombasa of a foreign-funded special piracy court and prison, means some Somalis perceive Kenya as an enemy.

Kenya has reason to be nervous. In September 2010, the Kenyan police leaked to the media documents containing details of an al-Qaeda cell in East Africa, which they accused of being behind the twin bomb attacks in Uganda. According to the leaked documents, dozens of young men in Kenya had joined the cell, had been trained in Somalia by al-Shabaab, and were planning an attack on Kenya. In November 2010, six young men were arrested in the coastal town of Lamu on suspicion of being al-Shabaab supporters on their way to fight in Somalia. Days after Kenyan troops entered Somalia in October 2011, one person was killed and many others injured in two grenade attacks in Nairobi. A Kenyan, who said he was a member of al-Shabaab, was sentenced to life imprisonment after he pleaded guilty to taking part in the attacks.

The authorities have to be vigilant, but they also have to be careful not to provoke the Somalis, especially as so many of them are citizens of Kenya or live there as refugees. Al-Shabaab has said it believes it can march on Nairobi without difficulty because Kenya is a pushover compared with Ethiopia, which is perceived as being far more militarized and authoritarian. Somalis joke that they need their army to fight Ethiopia, whereas Kenya can be easily dealt with by the police.

A United Nations report suggested Somali Islamism has taken deep root in Kenya:

> Kenya's large Somali community, its proximity to Somalia and the notoriously porous border between the two countries all contribute to Kenya's emergence as a major base of support for Somali armed opposition groups. Members of Shabaab and Hizbul Islam travel with relative freedom to and from Nairobi, where they raise funds, engage in recruitment and obtain treatment for wounded fighters. A key pillar of this support network is a community of wealthy clerics-cum-businessmen, linked to a small number of religious centres notorious for their links to radicalism ... The networks organized around these institutions have long provided both ideological leadership and a resource base for Somali militants.[23]

A 2009 US diplomatic cable, 'A portrait of *Al Shabaab* recruitment in Kenya', describes how the country has become 'a fruitful source for recruiting young men' to join groups such as al-Shabaab:

> An Isiolo businessman claims that sixty young Kenyan Somali men have disappeared from the town since January 2008 to fight in Somalia, and that two he knew personally recently died while conducting suicide bomb attacks in Mogadishu. Recruitment in Isiolo, he said, is directed from a radical mosque in Eastleigh but carried out by members of four radical mosques around Isiolo. Parents are grieving in private but are afraid of speaking out, he said. Even if the Kenyan government becomes actively involved in rooting out the recruitment network, there are no easy answers to this problem. We will continue to actively explore ways the United States can be of assistance.[24]

Such reports cause immense anger among many Somalis in Kenya, including the prominent Eastleigh-based businessman Sheikh Mohamed Ibrahim Shakul:

> We have heard many times about piracy money and terrorist money coming to Eastleigh. We need to clarify things, to put things into perspective. We raise our money from private investors and loans from Islamic banks. The stereotype that goes around in the media that there is piracy and terrorist money here is unfounded.
>
> I challenge anyone to show me a business here in Eastleigh that is based on illegal activity. I dare anyone to show me. We know with whom we are dealing. We know our stakeholders. Unfortunately, these claims are based on discrimination, on ethnic bias to target a specific community and its activities.
>
> I am not saying that everything that takes place in Eastleigh or in the Somali community is a hundred per cent OK as I don't have the ability or the knowledge to do so. But as a member of this community, deeply involved in people's livelihoods and their daily activities, I can assure you there is no such activity, or maybe very insignificant activity.

Other members of the Somali business community in Kenya have spoken of how they are exploited by the police. I spoke to a successful Somali businessman in his office in downtown Nairobi. He did not want to give his name: 'Do you know what the Kenyan police call Somalis? They call us ATM machines. That's because the only way we can navigate the situation here is to bribe the police at every turn.'

The businessman always uses the name of his non-Somali business partner in dealings with the authorities; a Somali identity, he says, is 'commercial suicide'. He has good reason to speak like this. Life is becoming increasingly difficult for Somalis in Kenya. They are treated with suspicion even though many of them are natives of the country. In central Nairobi, I watched every ethnic Somali – easily identified by the security guard by their distinctive physical features – being scanned with a metal detector and physically searched as they entered an office block; non-Somalis were left alone. In August 2010, the Central Bank of Kenya directed all financial institutions in the country to monitor the transactions of Kenya-based Somalis suspected of having links with Islamist insurgents in Somalia.

Prejudice against Somalis permeates many levels of Kenyan society. On the one hand, they are feared and resented; on the other, they are admired for their business acumen. The opinions of this taxi driver who drove me to Eastleigh reflect those of many others in the country: 'Somalis are very bad people. They sell everything in Eastleigh, even weapons. They are corrupt and they are always fighting because they are, by nature, a very violent people. Somali pirates come here to Nairobi and buy expensive houses in the best districts. Kenyans hate Somalis, but they are very good at business.'

The businessman Sheikh Shakul told me the entrepreneurial spirit of the Somalis brings great benefits to Kenya. I met him in his offices in a new mall he was building in Eastleigh, as the clatter of building work went on all around us:

> A business like this should be appreciated by everybody. It has created jobs, it will create revenue for the community and for the government. It will generate taxes. It has helped so many people – Kenyans, Somalis, and others.
>
> I think that Somalis are more of an asset than a burden to the Kenyan community because they create jobs. See how many people are working, just here in this building. I am providing hundreds of Kenyans with their daily bread. The government is collecting taxes from all the shops in Eastleigh. It is collecting revenue from all the customs duties paid on

goods imported by the Somalis. I believe the prejudice against Somalis is due to competition. Somalis have improved the lives of hundreds, if not millions, of Kenyans, giving them jobs as directors, accountants, maids, workmen, foremen and so on. We have to look at both sides of the story.

It may be their success in business rather than their links to piracy and Islamist extremism which lies at the root of Kenyan hostility towards Somalis. They were doing well in Kenya before the days of pirates and al-Shabaab. Nowhere is their commercial success more obvious than in Eastleigh, popularly known as 'Mogadishu Kidogo', Kiswahili for 'Mini-Mogadishu'. It is a riot of hotels and shopping malls. Dozens of large buildings are dedicated entirely to shopping: Day to Day Centre, Bangkok Shopping Mall, Prestige Centre, Towhid Shopping Complex, Emirates Shopping Mall, Olympic Shopping Centre, Sunrise Shopping Mall … The cheap prices and vast array of products attract shoppers from all over Kenya and elsewhere in East Africa. There are several new buildings under construction, some covered with marble and expensive reflective glass, others many storeys high.

Eastleigh is chaotic compared with the relative order of nearby downtown Nairobi, and its infrastructure is dilapidated. There are potholes everywhere and many of the roads are unpaved. Pedestrians have to navigate their way around open drains and mountains of uncollected rubbish. Electricity and water supplies are erratic. So bad is the provision of public services that in 2010 residents of Eastleigh stopped paying local taxes; their decision was endorsed by a court.

The Andalus Hotel, home to many of Somalia's exiled politicians, is attached to the Eastleigh Mall. Unlike many of the other shopping complexes, it is not a dark warren of endless kiosks, but a whole mini-world. It has a state-of-the-art gym, a medical centre, a restaurant, a bank and a mosque. There is the Star FM

11 Somali trader in an Eastleigh shopping mall (Mary Harper)

radio station, which broadcasts in Somali, and an Internet café, both essential for keeping in touch with news about Somalis at home and in the diaspora.

The dynamism of Eastleigh, the stability of Somaliland and the relative peace brought about by the Union of Islamic Courts are all examples of how Somalis can 'get it right' by operating largely on their own initiative and doing things their own way. The best hope for Somalia may be to follow a similar unconventional but specifically Somali route to stability. It would be naive to argue that these 'success stories' can be easily emulated or transposed to the whole of Somalia, but they show that there is a positive side to the Somali story, and they offer useful lessons, ideas and examples.

As it stands, Somalia represents one of today's most vexing challenges to international policy-makers. Foreign involvement in the conflict, whether through direct military action or otherwise, has so far been counterproductive. Leaving Somalia alone or keeping a distance has also proved unsuccessful. As growing numbers of Somalis from the diaspora return home to join violent Islamist movements, and possibly to plan attacks on foreign soil, the 'Somali problem' looks set to intensify and to become more globalized. For non-Somali Islamist extremists, Somalia is now high on the list of places where they want to go and fight.

CONCLUSION

The complexity and long duration of the conflict in Somalia, and the often counterproductive foreign interventions in the country, have left many inside and outside the country confused and, at times, afraid of what to do next. Portrayals of Somalia as the world's most comprehensively failed state,[1] inhabited by pirates, Islamist extremists and starving people, have exacerbated the problem and have, in all likelihood, contributed to many misguided policies.

Because Somalia has been labelled a 'failed', 'fragile' or 'collapsed' state, many policy-makers concluded that it represented a threat to global security. The association of 'state failure' with international terrorism became particularly strong after the events of 9/11. However, the perceived global threat posed by an ungoverned Somalia was initially exaggerated. This led to poor foreign policy decisions, which focused on what was dangerous and bad about the country, rather than what was positive and hopeful. The implementation of these decisions has in many ways created the monster which policy-makers fallaciously believed Somalia to be.

Approaches to Somalia were squeezed into the post-9/11 paradigm, leading to a blinkered perspective; Somalia became part of the 'War on Terror' narrative. Even before the fall of Siad Barre, Somalia was a difficult and, at times, dangerous place, but the collapse of central government did not automatically mean it became an instant threat to the Western world and a haven for Islamist extremists.

Outside observers have generally not realized that, while the central state was 'failing', and often *because* it was failing, Somalis devised some fascinating and exciting alternative ways of organizing society, some elements of which could be used as models for other countries experiencing war or other forms of disruption. The fact that many aspects of life in Somalia are unusual does not mean they are wrong, bad or threatening.

The more successful experiments in Somalia have been 'home grown', emerging from the grass roots of society, rather than being imposed from the outside. Bruton suggests that the United States should learn from these examples by distancing itself from Somalia: 'What can be termed "constructive disengagement" may appear to be a counterintuitive approach, but doing less is better than doing harm.'[2]

The Union of Islamic Courts' control of south-central Somalia and the self-declared republic of Somaliland in the north-west are two of the more interesting and potentially useful examples, but they should not be romanticized. Bradbury writes that one reason why Somaliland has not been taken seriously as a possible role model is that it does not fit into any conventional category of statehood or polity:

> Somaliland is one of several polities that have emerged since the end of the Cold War that do not fit into the normative world of juridical states and have been variously described as 'non-state entities', 'quasi-states' and 'states-within-states'. These political entities challenge the basis of international law and the territorial integrity of states, while their large diaspora communities are altering notions of citizenship and changing the relationship between states and their citizens, as well as the ways in which livelihoods are generated. For many people living in these non-states, the local political arrangements provide better security than was previously provided by formal state structures.

Somaliland challenges international efforts at state-building in Somalia, by questioning the basis for and the nature of that state and by demonstrating an alternative route to state-building than has been determined by foreign diplomats and aid programmes to date.[3]

One of the biggest 'failures' of policy towards Somalia has been the fixation with lengthy and expensive internationally sponsored 'peace conferences', held outside the country. There have to date been nearly twenty such meetings, none of them successful. They have produced a succession of weak transitional governments, all of which have so far ended in failure. These governments have controlled limited parts of the country; their authority has sometimes extended to no more than a few blocks of the capital, Mogadishu. They have paid lip-service to the principle of federalism, but they have tended to be highly centralized, with the focus of authority concentrated in Mogadishu. Sometimes the administrations have been based in other Somali towns, or even outside the country, because of the fighting and the intense hatred their presence has generated in the capital. They lack popular legitimacy because many Somalis see them as foreign creations. These governments have found it impossible to defeat their enemies, partly because the conflict is so fractured and complex. A United Nations report of 2010 vividly describes the situation:

The conflict remains a grim example of 'hybrid warfare': a combination of conventional capabilities, irregular tactics and formations, as well as indiscriminate violence, coercion and criminal disorder – compounded in the Somali case by the interference of regional powers. Somalia's frail Transitional Federal Government has struggled ineffectually to contain a complex insurgency that conflates religious extremism, political and financial opportunism, and clan interests.[4]

Western powers, particularly the USA and Britain, had by 2010 adopted a revised approach towards Somalia. They continued to support and recognize the transitional government in Mogadishu but gave increased attention to more stable areas, especially Puntland and Somaliland. They adopted this 'dual track' approach twenty years after the fall of central government. This was probably too late to have much of an impact on the southern and central regions of the country, where conflict had become endemic.

Foreign governments are at last starting to support the more stable regions of Somali territory; they could also focus more closely on the positive developments in those parts of the country worst affected by conflict. These include the extraordinary growth of some parts of the economy, both traditional and modern. A great deal could be learned from the dramatic success of the livestock trade during the years of conflict, and the spectacular development of new sectors, such as telecommunications. One reason for this is the absence of state interference or control.

The Somalis are dynamic and have boldly adopted modern technology. As a result, despite and because of years of war and state 'failure', they are making a significant economic impact on many parts of Africa and elsewhere. Their energetic embrace of the Internet and mobile telephony has enabled Somalis to participate wholeheartedly in the global economy even though they are in many ways a stateless people. They have been scattered all over the world, but they remain a coherent economic force. They are fully linked to local, regional and international trade and financial networks, whether in the traditional livestock trade or the modern money transfer business. It is as if the Somali community somehow floats above the world, having reached a postmodern stage of development, beyond the nation-state.

One reason why Somalis have managed to do so well without a strong central government is that their traditional way of life does not fit well with statehood. The idea of a nation-state is not very useful for Somalis. They have their own way of organizing themselves; international policy-makers should not be alarmed by or dismissive of what may seem a chaotic, 'horizontal' way of doing politics. The pastoral, clan-based lineage system was in place long before the colonial powers imposed themselves on Somalia, and worked as an effective way of governing society. Somalis have for centuries effectively interacted and traded with more centralized powers, in the Arab world, South Asia and Europe.

For more than twenty years, outside powers have struggled to sort out the problem of Somalia. Military interventions, humanitarian operations and diplomacy have failed to bring about lasting positive change in the country. Perhaps, like the Somalis themselves, the approach needs to be more creative and adventurous. The rest of the world also needs to recognize that Somalis can be very good at doing things for themselves.

NOTES

Introduction

1 www.foreignpolicy.com/failed-states (last accessed August 2011).

2 Antonio Guterres, United Nations High Commissioner for Refugees, July 2011.

3 www.transparency.org/policy_research/surveys_indices/cpi/2010/results (last accessed August 2011).

4 *Economist*, 371, 2004, p. 58.

5 This phrase occurs frequently in media reports; for example, Peter Hughes, *Daily Telegraph*, 13 May 2011.

6 www.foreignpolicy.com/articles/2009/02/16/the_most_dangerous_place_in_the_world (last accessed August 2011), www.bbc.co.uk/news/uk-politics-14558721 (last accessed August 2011).

7 Richard Burton, *First Footsteps in East Africa* (New York: Dover, 1987 [1856]), vol. 1, p. 122.

8 Ioan Lewis, *Understanding Somalia and Somaliland* (London: Hurst and Co., 2008), p. 25.

9 James Rennell Rodd, *Social and Diplomatic Memories 1894–1901*, 1923.

10 Scott Peterson, *Me Against My Brother* (New York: Routledge, 2002), p. 1.

1 Clan and country

1 Richard Dowden, *Africa: Altered States, Ordinary Miracles* (London: Portobello, 2008), p. 93.

2 www.facebook.com/#!/pages/Somali-Camel/111689282692 (last accessed January 2011).

3 John Drysdale, *The Somali Dispute* (New York: Praeger, 1964), p. 10.

4 Ioan Lewis, *A Modern History of Somalia* (Oxford: James Currey, 2002), p. 8.

5 Martin Murphy, *Somalia: The New Barbary?* (London: Hurst and Co., 2011), p. 18.

6 Ioan Lewis, *Understanding Somalia and Somaliland* (London: Hurst and Co., 2008), p. 3.

7 Ibid., p. 56.

8 Lewis, *A Modern History of Somalia*, p. 10.

9 Michael Walls, 'The emergence of a Somali state', *African Affairs*, 108(432), 2009, p. 377.

10 Nuruddin Farah, *From a Crooked Rib* (London: Heinemann, 1970), p. 13.

11 Nuruddin Farah, *Gifts* (Cape Town: Kwela Books, 2001), p. 197.

12 Lewis, *Understanding Somalia and Somaliland*, p. 23.

13 B. W. Andrzejewski and Sheila Andrzejewski, *An Anthology of Somali Poetry* (Bloomington: Indiana University Press, 1993), p. 32.

14 Ibid., p. 78.

15 www.bbc.co.uk/news/world-africa-12246627 (last accessed August 2011). To see Abdirashid

Omar performing his poem in Somali, visit www.youtube.com/watch?v=MrXh3ceV_MA.

16 For a detailed account of Somali nicknames, see 'Somali (nick) names and their meanings' by Markus Hoehne with Muuse Cali Faruur and Axmed Cabdullahi Du'aale in Markus Hoehne and Virginia Luling (eds), *Peace and Milk, Drought and War* (London: Hurst and Co., 2010), pp. 345–63.

17 Part of this interview was originally broadcast on the BBC World Service in 2011. Some quotes in the book have been broadcast in programmes I have made for the BBC; others are original material.

18 Lewis, *A Modern History of Somalia*, p. 1.

19 UNDP, *Somalia's Missing Million: The Somali Diaspora and Its Role in Development*, 2009.

20 Virginia Luling, 'Genealogy as theory, genealogy as tool: aspect of Somali "clanship"', *Social Identities: Journal for the Study of Race, Nation and Culture*, 12(4), July 2006.

21 Drysdale, *The Somali Dispute*, p. 8.

22 Lewis, *Understanding Somalia and Somaliland*, p. 23.

2 History

1 John Drysdale, *The Somali Dispute* (London: Pall Mall Press, 1964), p. 21.

2 Ioan Lewis, *A Modern History of Somalia* (Oxford: James Currey, 2002), p. 5.

3 Harold Nelson (ed.), *Somalia: A Country Study* (Washington, DC: American University Press, 1982), p. 7.

4 Tom J. Farer, *War Clouds on the Horn of Africa: A Crisis for Détente* (New York: Carnegie, 1976), p. 54.

5 War Office, *Official History of the Operations in Somaliland*, vol. 1, 1907, p. 192.

6 Abdi Sheikh-Abdi, *Divine Madness* (London: Zed Books, 1993), p. 55.

7 Douglas Jardine, *The Mad Mullah of Somaliland* (London: H. Jenkins, 1923), p. 249.

8 Sheikh-Abdi, *Divine Madness*, p. 77.

9 Farer, *War Clouds on the Horn of Africa*, p. 62.

10 B. W. Andrzejewski and I. M. Lewis, *Somali Poetry: An Introduction* (Oxford: Clarendon Press, 1964), p. 57.

11 Dr Abdirashid Ali Sharmarke, *The Somali Peninsula: A New Light on Imperial Motives*, London, 1962.

12 *The Issue of the Northern Frontier District*, White Paper issued by the Somali government, Mogadishu, 1963.

13 Drysdale, *The Somali Dispute*, p. 162.

14 Sir Gerald Reece, *The British Survey*, Main Series no. 98 (London: Colonial Office, 1952), quoted in Said Samatar, *Somalia: Nation in Search of a State* (Boulder, CO: Westview Press, 1987).

15 Iqbal Jhazbhay, *Somaliland: An African Struggle for Nationhood and International Recognition* (South Africa: Institute for Global Dialogue and South African Institute for International Affairs, 2009), p. 13.

16 Ioan Lewis, *Making and Breaking States in Africa* (Lawrenceville, NJ: Red Sea Press, 2010), p. 89.

17 Mark Bradbury, *Becoming Somaliland* (London: Progressio, 2008), p. 73.

18 Ibid., p. 48.

19 Ibid., p. 92.

20 United Nations Monitoring Group report, 10 March 2010.

21 Said Samatar, in Markus Hoehne and Virginia Luling (eds), *Milk and Peace, Drought and War* (London: Hurst and Co., 2010), p. 217.

3 Islamism

1 Human Rights Watch, *Harsh War, Harsh Peace*, April 2010, www.hrw.org/reports/2010/04/13/harsh-war-harsh-peace (last accessed August 2011).

2 Ioan Lewis, *Saints and Somalis: Popular Islam in a Clan-based Society* (London: Haan, 1998), p. 25.

3 Stig Jarle Hansen and Atle Mesoy, *The Muslim Brotherhood in the Wider Horn of Africa*, NIBR, p. 40, www.nibr.no/uploads/publications/06d76b6e0d14594c9a753c487ed50e51.pdf (last accessed August 2011).

4 International Crisis Group, *Somalia's Islamists*, 2005, p. 1, www.crisisgroup.org/en/regions/africa/horn-of-africa/somalia/100-somalias-islamists.aspx (last accessed August 2011).

5 Ibid., p. 7.

6 Ken Menkhaus, *Somalia: State Collapse and the Threat of Terrorism*, IISS Adelphi Paper 364, p. 56.

7 Roland Marchal, 'Somalia: a new front against terrorism', SSRC blog, 2007, www.hornofafrica.ssrc.org/marchal/index1.html (last accessed August 2011).

8 Cedric Barnes and Harun Hassan, *The Rise and Fall of Mogadishu's Islamic Courts*, Chatham House, 2007, www.chathamhouse.org/publications/papers/view/108453 (last accessed August 2011).

9 Quoted in Anna Lindley, 'Leaving Mogadishu: towards a sociology of conflict-related mobility', *Journal of Refugee Studies*, 2010.

10 Al-Shabaab statement, February 2010.

11 UN Panel of Experts report, 2010, p. 6, www.un.org/ga/search/view_doc.asp?symbol=S/2010/91 (last accessed March 2011).

12 IRIN, April 2010.

13 UN Panel of Experts report, 2010, p. 30.

14 Andrea Elliot, 'A call to jihad, answered in America', *New York Times*, 12 July 2009.

15 FBI report, 2009.

16 FBI report, 2010.

17 Ibid.

18 Elliot, 'A call to jihad'.

4 A failed state?

1 www.foreignpolicy.com/failed-states (last accessed August 2011).

2 Noam Chomsky, *Failed States: The Abuse of Power and the Assault on Democracy* (New York: Metropolitan, 2006).

3 Robert I. Rotberg, 'The new nature of nation-state failure', *Washington Quarterly*, 25(3), 2002, p. 85.

4 Ian Birrell, 'It's time the world listened to new stories out of Africa', *Observer*, 20 February 2011.

5 Peter Little, *Somalia: Economy without State* (Oxford and Bloomington: James Currey and Indiana University Press, 2003), p. xv.

6 Benjamin Powell, Ryan Ford and Alex Nowrasteh, 'Somalia after state collapse: chaos or improvement?', Independent Institute, November 2006.

7 Ibid.

8 Peter Leeson, *Better Off Stateless: Somalia before and after state collapse*, West Virginia University, 2006.

9 www.unhcr.org/4ca602a66.html (last accessed August 2011).

10 Little, *Somalia: Economy without State*, p. 8.

11 Anna Lindley, 'Between "dirty money" and "development capital"', *African Affairs*, August 2009, p. 528.

12 Little, *Somalia: Economy without State*, p. 166.

13 Ibid., p. 37.

14 Ibid., p. 91.

15 Ibid., p. 131.

16 Lindley, 'Between "dirty money" and "development capital"', p. 539.

17 *Focus on Africa*, April–June 2011.

18 Lindley, 'Between "dirty money" and "development capital"', p. 523.

19 news.bbc.co.uk/1/hi/world/africa/4020259.stm (last accessed August 2011).

20 Mark Bradbury, *Becoming Somaliland* (London: Progressio, 2008), p. 1.

21 Iqbal Jhazbhay, *Somaliland: An African Struggle for Nationhood and International Recognition* (South Africa: Institute for Global Dialogue and South African Institute for International Affairs, 2009), p. 14.

22 Bradbury, *Becoming Somaliland*, p. 93.

23 Ibid., p. 106.

24 Ibid., p. 242.

25 Michael Walls, 'The emergence of a Somali state', *African Affairs*, 108(432), 2009, p. 389.

26 Rageh Omaar, 'The jihadists next door', *Guardian*, 6 July 2010.

5 Piracy

1 There is a growing range of novels inspired by Somali piracy, as well as first-hand accounts of people held hostage by pirates. These include: Paul and Rachel Chandler with Sarah Edworthy, *Hostage: A Year at Gunpoint with Somali Gangsters* (Edinburgh: Mainstream, 2011), Colin Freeman, *Kidnapped: Life as a Somali Pirate Hostage* (Wolvey: Monday, 2011), and Elmore Leonard, *Djibouti* (London: Weidenfeld and Nicolson, 2011).

2 business.timesonline.co.uk/tol/business/industry_sectors/banking_and_finance/article4727372.ece (last accessed August 2011).

3 Ecoterra International Counter-Piracy Updates.

4 oneearthfuture.org/images/imagefiles/The%20Economic%20Cost %20of%20Piracy%20Full%20 Report.pdf (last accessed November 2011).

5 news.bbc.co.uk/1/hi/7824353.stm (last accessed August 2011); www.guardian.co.uk/world/2009/jan/10/sirius-star-somalia-pirates-drown (last accessed August 2011).

6 Stig Jarle Hansen, *Piracy in the Greater Gulf of Aden: Myths, Misconceptions and Remedies*, NIBR, 2009, p. 12.

7 Ibid., p. 8.

8 news.bbc.co.uk/1/hi/world/africa/8061535.stm (last accessed August 2011).

9 Jeffrey Gettleman, 'Somalia's pirates flourish in a lawless nation', *New York Times*, 30 October 2008.

10 Ibid.

11 United Nations Security Council report, March 2010, p. 39.

12 AP, November 2008.

13 Ibid.

14 Press conference, US embassy, London, February 2011.

15 Hansen, *Piracy in the Greater Gulf of Aden*, p. 41.

16 Ibid., p. 34.

17 The information on codes of conduct was obtained during research I conducted in July and August 2011 for the Small Arms Survey monitoring group.

18 Reuters, November 2008.

19 Ibid.

20 BBC, April 2009.

21 Colin Freeman, 'Somali pirates on trial in Holland', *Daily Telegraph*, 13 June 2010.

22 Ibid.

23 Kaija Hulburt, *The Human Cost of Somali Piracy*, June 2011, p. 13, oceansbeyondpiracy.org/cost-of-piracy/human-cost-somali-piracy (last accessed August 2011).

24 Ibid., p. 17.

25 Ibid., p. 17.

26 Dipendra Rathore, 'Experience: I was kidnapped by Somali pirates', *Guardian*, 11 June 2011.

27 www.marad.dot.gov/documents/EUNAVFOR_Surviving_Piracy_Seafarers_Leaflet_v2.pdf (last accessed August 2011).

28 Hansen, *Piracy in the Greater Gulf of Aden*, p. 30.

6 Somalia and the outside world

1 Anna Lindley, 'Between "dirty money" and "development capital"', *African Affairs*, 108(433), 2009, p. 539.

2 BBC, 3 September 2010.

3 The term was invented by the *Washington Post* columnist Jim Hoagland to describe the US intervention in Somalia in 1993.

4 White House press release, Washington, DC, 7 November 2001.

5 The National Security Strategy of the United States, White House, September 2002.

6 The National Security Strategy of the United States, White House, March 2006.

7 Markus Virgil Hoehne, African Arguments blog, SSRC, 2009, hornofafrica.ssrc.org/somalia/ (last accessed August 2011).

8 Bronwyn Bruton, *Somalia: A New Approach*, Council on Foreign Relations, 2010, p. 8.

9 BBC, 13 September 2011.

10 Ibid., p. 19.

11 United Nations Monitoring Group report, 10 March 2010, p. 6.

12 US diplomatic cable, 'Somalia – TFG prime minister worried about rival organization, anxious for USG help', Wikileaks, 2009.

13 Chris Mullin, *A View from the Foothills* (London: Profile, 2009), p. 503.

14 United Nations Monitoring Group report, 10 March 2010, p. 54.

15 Jeffrey Gettleman, Mark Mazzetti and Eric Schmitt, 'U.S. relies on contractors in Somalia conflict', *New York Times*, 10 August 2011.

16 US diplomatic cable, 'Carter informed that UK to increase Somalia engagement', Wikileaks, 2009.

17 Markus Virgil Hoehne, Africa Arguments blog, SSRC, 2009, hornofafrica.ssrc.org/somalia/ (last accessed August 2011).

18 United Nations Monitoring Group report, 10 March 2010, p. 7.

19 Ibid., p. 24.

20 US diplomatic cable, 'An Eritrean overture to the United States', Wikileaks, 2009.

21 Human Rights Watch, *Welcome to Kenya*, June 2010.

22 US diplomatic cable, 'A portrait of *Al Shabaab* recruitment in Kenya', Wikileaks, 2009.

23 United Nations Monitoring Group report, 10 March 2010, p. 25.

24 US diplomatic cable, 'A portrait of *Al Shabaab* recruitment in Kenya', Wikileaks, 2009.

Conclusion

1 International Crisis Group, *Somalia: To Move Beyond the Failed State*, 2008.

2 Bronwyn Bruton, *Somalia: A New Approach*, Council on Foreign Relations, 2010, p. 5.

3 Mark Bradbury, *Becoming Somaliland* (London: Progressio, 2008), p. 6.

4 United Nations Monitoring Group report, 10 March 2010, p. 6.

BIBLIOGRAPHY

Ali, A. H. (2007) *Infidel*, London: Simon and Schuster.

Andrzejewski, B. W. and S. Andrzejewski (1993) *An Anthology of Somali Poetry*, Bloomington: Indiana University Press.

Andrzejewski, B. W. and I. M. Lewis (1964) *Somali Poetry: An Introduction*, Oxford: Clarendon Press.

Bowden, M. (1999) *Black Hawk Down: A Story of Modern War*, New York: Atlantic Monthly Press.

Bradbury, M. (2008) *Becoming Somaliland*, London: Progressio.

Chomsky, N. (2006) *Failed States: The Abuse of Power and the Assault on Democracy*, New York: Metropolitan.

De Waal, A. (2004) *Islamism and Its Enemies in the Horn of Africa*, London: Hurst and Co.

Dowden, R. (2008) *Africa: Altered States, Ordinary Miracles*, London: Portobello.

Drysdale, J. (1964) *The Somali Dispute*, New York: Praeger.

— (1994) *Whatever Happened to Somalia*, London: Haan.

Elmi, A. E. (2010) *Understanding the Somali Conflagration*, London: Pluto.

Farah, N. (1970) *A Crooked Rib*, London: Heinemann.

— (1986) *Maps*, London: Penguin.

— (1998) *Secrets*, New York: Arcade.

— (2001) *Gifts*, Cape Town: Kwela Books.

Farer, T. (1976) *War Clouds on the Horn of Africa: A Crisis for Détente*, New York: Carnegie.

Hoehne, M. and V. Luling (eds) (2010) *Peace and Milk, Drought and War*, London: Hurst and Co.

International Crisis Group has some excellent reports on Somalia, www.crisisgroup.org/en/regions/africa/horn-of-africa/somalia.aspx (last accessed August 2011).

Jardine, D. (1923) *The Mad Mullah of Somaliland*, London: H. Jenkins.

Jhazbhay, I. (2009) *Somaliland: An African Struggle for Nationhood and International Recognition*, South Africa: Institute for Global Dialogue and South African Institute for International Affairs.

Leonard, E. (2011) *Djibouti*, London: Weidenfeld and Nicolson.

Lewis, I. (1961) *A Pastoral Democracy*, Oxford: James Currey.

— (1998) *Saints and Somalis: Popular Islam in a Clan-based Society*, London: Haan.

— (2002 [1980]) *A Modern History of Somalia*, Oxford: James Currey.

— (2008) *Understanding Somalia and Somaliland*, London: Hurst and Co.

— (2010) *Making and Breaking States in Africa*, Lawrenceville, NJ: Red Sea Press.

Lindley, A. (2010) *The Early Morning Phone Call: Somali Refugees' Remittances*, New York: Berghahn Books.

Little, P. (2003) *Somalia: Economy without State*, Oxford and Bloomington: James Currey and Indiana University Press.

Menkhaus, K. (2004) *Somalia: State Collapse and the Threat of Terrorism*, International Institute for Strategic Studies and Oxford University Press.

Mohamed, N. (2010) *Black Mamba Boy*, London: HarperCollins.

Mullin, C. (2009) *A View from the Foothills*, London: Profile.

Murphy, M. (2011) *Somalia: The New Barbary?*, London: Hurst and Co.

Nelson, H. (ed.) (1982) *Somalia: A Country Study*, Washington, DC: American University Press.

Omaar, R. (2006) *Only Half of Me*, London: Viking.

Peterson, S. (2002) *Me Against My Brother*, New York: Routledge.

Samatar, A. (1994a) *Socialist Somalia: Rhetoric and Reality*, London: Zed Books.

— (ed.) (1994b) *The Somali Challenge: From Catastrophe to Renewal?*, Boulder, CO: Lynne Rienner.

Samatar, S. (1987) *Somalia: A Nation in Search of a State*, Boulder, CO: Westview Press.

— (1991) *Somalia: A Nation in Turmoil*, London: Minority Rights Group.

Sheikh-Abdi, A. (1993) *Divine Madness*, London: Zed Books.

INDEX

11 September 2001 attacks, 169

Abdi, Mohamed (Professor Gandhi), 110
Abdirahman, a Somali boy refugee, 92
Abgal sub-clan, 42, 57
Adam, Abdiweli Mohamed, 90–1
'Adan', a pirate, 150
Adan, Mohamed, 110
Aden, British base in, 47
adoon, use of term, 16
'Adowe', a pirate, 162
Afewerki, Isaias, 187
Afghanistan, 9, 82, 83; 'Great Game', 6
Afgoye Corridor, 113
Africa Orientale Italiana, 50
African Union (AU), 34, 61, 64, 71, 89,
    107, 108, 126, 132, 175–6
African Union Mission in Somalia
    (AMISOM), 95
agriculture, 19
Ahlu Sunna wa Jamaa, 40, 85, 180
Ahmed, Sheikh Sharif Sheikh, 97, 172,
    174
Ahmed, Shirwa, 99
Ahmediya brotherhood, 75
Ahzari, Al, 89, 95, 97
aid agencies, 184
aid assistance, 175; challenge of, 181–4
    see also humanitarian aid
Aideed, Mohamed Farah, 6, 42, 61, 62
Albright, Madeleine, 62
alcohol, addiction to, 155
Ali, Gedow, 142–3, 149
Alliance for the Re-liberation of
    Somalia, 66

Alliance for the Restoration of Peace
    and Counter-Terrorism (ARPCT),
    36, 80, 170
Andalus Hotel (Eastleigh, Kenya),
    194–5
ankles, required showing of, 73
Arab world, connections with, 45
Australia, 27; Somali plot uncovered
    in, 102
Aweys, Hassan Dahir, 33, 42, 76, 78,
    82, 93–4, 98, 187; interview with,
    87–8
Ayr sub-clan, 42, 82
Ayro, Adan Hashi, 42, 82–3, 173; death
    of, 180

Bakara market, Mogadishu, shelling
    of, 61
bananas, in diet, 19
Bancroft Global Development, 178
banking, pavement banks, 121
Bantu minority, 16
Barakat, al-, company, 123; closure
    of, 181; put onto US terrorism list,
    168–9
Barnes, Cedric, 81
Barre, Mohamed Suleiman, 102
BBC World Service, Somali-language
    broadcasts, 26, 38
beards, forced growing of, 73
bells in school, banning of, 92
Berbera, port, 126
Bevin, Ernest, plan for Somalia, 50–1
Birrell, Ian, 107
Black Hawk Down, 61; film, 6–7

Blair, Dennis, 100
Blair, Tony, 166–7
blood money, payment of, 17, 40, 115
Bollywood movies, used for suicide
     bombing training, 90
borders, maintenance of, 132
Boroma conference (1993), 133–4
Boutros-Ghali, Boutros, 167
bow and arrow shooting,
     encouragement of, 72–3
Bradbury, Mark, 62–3, 125–6, 133–4,
     198; *Becoming Somaliland*, 56
brain drain, to aid organizations, 139
British Protectorate of Somaliland, 12,
     47, 49, 56
Bruton, Bronwyn, 173–5, 198
Burton, Richard, 6
Burundi, 176, 184–5
Bush, George, 62
Bush, George W., 79, 168, 181
business activities of Somalis, 115–16

camels, 16, 21, 26, 28, 47; milk of, 18,
     22; role of, in local culture, 17–18
Carson, Johnnie, 96, 177
Center for Combating Terrorism
     (USA), 171
Central Bank of Kenya, 193
central government, 65; absence of, 8,
     59, 64, 66, 111, 113, 116, 117, 119 (not
     an obstacle, 200; positive aspects
     of, 115); collapse of, 3, 4, 43, 56–9,
     106; obstacles to, 11; resistance
     to, 22
Central Intelligence Agency (CIA),
     80; helps build base at Mogadishu
     airport, 178
Chandler, Paul, kidnap of, 110, 162
Chandler, Rachel, kidnap of, 110, 162
charcoal exports, banning of, 82
child soldiers, 1, 91
children, induction of, 90
Chomsky, Noam, 106
Christians, 16

civil war in Somalia, 56–60; as
     restructuring programme, 115
clan system, 57, 119, 123, 133, 139, 201;
     inherent divisiveness of, 11–12;
     stronger than government, 11
clans, 34, 35–43; as fighting groups,
     42; banning of, 41, 42, 54; family
     mapping of, 37; moves against, 40;
     naming of, 39; role of, 36
Clinton, Bill, 61
coast guards: training of, 159; use of
     term, 142, 149
coffee, trading of, 46
common law system, 112
Congo, Democratic Republic of,
     telephony in, 124
contracts, enforcement of, 82
Corfield, Richard, 48
corruption, 1
Côte Française des Somalis, 49
council of elders, 134
country, concept of, not meaningful,
     22
Crisis States Research Centre, 106
Cullen, Patrick, 158
customary law, 120

Dahabshiil company, 120, 122–3, 129
Dahir, a pirate, 149–50
Dahir, Sahra Sheikh, 154
dairy farming, 129–30
Darod clan, 12, 39, 41
data, impossibility of gathering
     information, 113
Davies, Chris, 160
Daybed, a pirate, 147–8
democracy, 88, 136
DHL company, 117
Dhulbahante sub-clan, 41
diaspora, 74, 95, 98, 99, 109, 125, 127,
     129, 196; trading in, 10, 21
Dir clan, 39
displaced persons, 113
diya see blood money

Djibouti, 31, 184
Dole Fruit company, 117
dowry, payment of, 17
dress, of fighters, 73
drought, 55
Drysdale, John, 18, 39, 44, 53
Duale, Abdirashid, 121, 123–4
Duale, Mohamed Said, 120–1

Eastleigh (Nairobi, Kenya), 29, 91, 92,
    114, 155, 191–2, 193–5; known as
    'mini-Mogadishu', 194
economy of Somalia, 111–17
Egal, Mohamed Ibrahim, 128, 133, 135
'Eid, Farah Ismail', 153
elections, 52, 53, 136
Elixh, Ismail, 151
Elmi, Abdulkader Hashi, 127–30
Eritrea, 51, 83, 172, 185–7
Ethiopia, 7, 31, 46, 49, 50, 51, 59, 79, 83,
    170, 176, 184, 185–7, 190–1; invasion
    of Somalia, 4, 103, 171–4, 180;
    Region Five, 49; war with, 4, 33, 55,
    83; withdrawal from Somalia, 180
European Union (EU), 64; *Surviving
    Piracy off the Coast of Somalia*, 164
executions, enforced watching of, 90

Failed State Index, 105
failed states, 105–41; definition of, 106;
    Somalia described as, 1, 4, 5, 197–8
    see also state failure
family legislation, 76
famine, 2, 59, 182–3
Farah, Abdullah, 17, 129–30
Farah, Nuruddin: *From a Crooked Rib*,
    24; *Gifts*, 24–5
Farer, Tom, 46–7, 49
Federal Bureau of Investigation (FBI),
    Operation Rhino, 100
films, watching of, in public parlours,
    banned, 10, 72
fish: rejected as diet, 19–20, 19;
    resources of, 19, 128 (foreign

trawling of, 142, 148–50; hostages
    perceived as, 149)
fishermen mistaken for pirates, 151
football: banning of, 72; watching of,
    forbidden in public parlours, 10,
    72, 92
foreign fighters, 97–102
foreigners, terms for, 28–9
France, 7, 46, 51
frankincense, 18, 46
Frazer, Jendayi, 172, 174, 187
frontiers, artificial, 52
Fund for Peace, 105

genealogies, recitation of, 39
General Motors of Kenya, 117
girls, unequal treatment of, 24
Godane, Ahmed Abdi (Abu Zubair),
    77, 86, 137, 181
Gortney, William, 158
government documents, misuse of,
    58
Greater Somalia, 12, 30–5, 49, 53, 55,
    75, 86
Guantánamo prison, 102–3
guns: AK-47, 89 (as quiz prize, 90);
    availability of, 193; children
    playing with, 67; omnipresence
    of, 57–8, 127, 128; provided by
    US government, 177; UN arms
    embargo, 155–6

Habr Gedir sub-clan, 42, 57, 62
hand-shaking between men and
    women, banned, 93
Hansen, Stig Jarle, 150, 156–7, 164
Hargeisa, 126, 137, 140; bombing of, 56
Hart Security company, 158
Hassan, a pirate, 149, 152
Hassan, Harun, 81
Hassan, Seyyid Mohamed Abdulle
    ('Mad Mullah'), 7–8, 32, 47–8, 49,
    75, 167; *A Land of Drought*, 26
Hassan, Yonis, 36

hawala money system, 119, 152
Hawiye clan, 39, 42, 56–7
hijab see women, veiling of
Hizbul Islam, 40, 77, 85, 158
Hoehne, Markus Virgil, 170–1, 180
Holder, Eric, 100
homogeneity of Somali population, 10, 15, 34, 53
Hopkins, Donna Lee, 156
Horn of Africa, 14, 31, 126, 140, 184
hospitals, maternity hospital in Hargeisa, 130–1
House of Elders, 40
Howe, Jonathan, 61
humanitarian assistance: aid agencies doing deals, 63; aid ships shot at, 59; diversion of, 183
humanitarian intervention, 6, 167
Hussein, Abdullahi Mohamed, 124
Hussein, Omar, 'Ostreeliya', *In Praise of Weris*, 27
Huureh, Ismail Mohamed (Booba), 139, 176–7
hybrid warfare, 199

'Ilkajiir', Abdullahi Ahmed Jama, 154
incense, production of, 18–19
Independent Institute, 112
infant mortality, 112
International Crisis Group, 77, 78
International Maritime Bureau, 145
Internet, 130; Islamist extremism on, 101; love of, among Somalis, 95; Somali-related websites, 26; usage of, 10, 33, 77, 195, 200
irrigation, 130
Isaq clan, 43, 55
Islah, al-, 77
Islam, 9; penetration of, 46; political, 76; seen as transcending clans, 77; Sunni, 74; Wahhabi, 77
Islamic courts *see* sharia courts
Islamic Salvation Front (FIS) (Algeria), 173

Islamism: development of, in Somalia, 70, 71–104; growth of, 180–7; radical, links with pirates, 157–8
Islamist groups, 34
Ismail, Aden, 30
Ismail, Edna Adan, 130
Italy, 7, 46, 50, 52
Itihaad al-Islamiyya, al-, 77–9; put onto US terrorism list, 168

Jareer minority, 16
Jerusalem, 86
jihad, 7, 47, 75, 86, 92, 101; import and export of, 96–104
Jimale, Ahmed Ali, 168
Johar, Abdi Waheed, 154
Joint Terrorism Task Force (Minneapolis, USA), 99
Jones, B. Todd, 100
Jubaland offensive, 189
Justice and Development party, 135–6

Kahin, Dahir Riyale, 135
Kataib, al-, television channel, 94–5
Kenya, 29, 31, 50, 64, 179, 184, 188–96; and livestock trade, 16; difficulties for Somalis in, 192–3; Islamism in, 191; Northern Frontier District, 49, 52; policy on piracy suspects, 161; secession from, 52–3; trading links with, 10 (in livestock, 118)
K'naan, a singer, 28

Laden, Osama bin, 83, 168, 172; killing of, 97; message on Somalia, 97
Land of Punt, 46
Leeson, Peter, 113
legislature, of Somaliland, 134
Lewis, Ioan, 7, 18, 21–2, 26, 39–40, 45, 54–5, 75
life expectancy, 112
Lindley, Anna, 115, 120, 166
literacy, campaigns, 12, 54–5
litter in Somaliland, 30

Little, Peter, 117–18; *Somalia: Economy without a State*, 111
livestock: export of, 47; rearing of, 22, 130; trading of, 16, 111, 117–19
Luling, Virginia, 38–9, 134
Luq, bombing of, 79

Majerteen clan, 41
Malele, a *qat* chewer, 30
Malloch Brown, Mark, 102
Marchal, Roland, 80
Marehan sub-clan, 41
Mariam, Aisha, 36
Marida Marguerite, MV, 163
marriage, 23; rising price of, 155
martyrdom, 83, 98
maternity services, lack of, 25
Mazrui, Ali, 126
Mengistu Haile Mariam, 55
Menkhaus, Ken, 78
mini-states, semi-autonomous, 109–10
Minneapolis, Somali community in, 99, 100
minority groups, 15–16
Moalimuu, Mohamed, 67–8
mobile phone systems, 2, 8, 10, 23, 33, 77, 119–25, 175–6
mobile phones: adoption of, 124–5; musical ring tones banned, 71, 92; use of, 200
Mogadishu, 34, 71, 87, 101, 108, 114, 124, 126, 199; bombing of, 171 (by Ethiopia, 83); death toll in, 69; destruction of, 58; displaced persons in, 113, 175; divided city, 42; insecurity in, 176; killings in, 107; refugee camps in, 173; security in, 81
Mogadishu play, 1
Mohamed, a Somali boy refugee, 91
Mohamed, Ali Mahdi, 42, 79
Mohamed, Fazul Abdullah, 84, 103
Mohamed, Mohamed, 22

Mohamed, Omar, 36
Mohamed, Omer Abdi, 100
monetary system, non-state, 112
money laundering, 123
money transfer systems, 2, 8, 33, 119–25, 152
Murphy, Martin, 20
Museveni, Yoweri, 136
music, banning of, 72; on radio stations, 92
Muslim Brotherhood, 76
Mussolini, Benito, 50
Muxamed, Muxamed Ibrahim, 37
Mwangura, Andrew, 152
myrrh, production of, 18, 46

nation state: concept of, 201; obstacles to, 36
nationalism, 75
nicknames, use of, 28–9
Nishky, Marek, 148
nomadism: idealization of, 21; relation to development of businesses, 115–16
nomads, 21–5, 31, 53, 117–19; as natural soldiers, 23; recruited by al-Shabaab, 118
non-governmental organizations (NGOs), 138
Northern Frontier District *see* Kenya, Northern Frontier District
Norwegian Institute for Urban and Regional Research (NIBR), 76
Nur, Faarah, 50
Nur, Yusuf, 36

Obama, Barack, 179, 181, 186
occupational groups, 16
Ogaden, 49, 51, 55
Ogaden National Liberation Front, 78
Ogaden sub-clan, 41
oil and gas reserves, 19
Omaar, Rageh, 140
Omar, Abdirashid, *Fatwo*, 27

One Earth Future Foundation, 145;
    report on piracy, 162
Operation Restore Hope, 60, 61
oral culture, 7, 26–9, 53, 125
oratory, 26

Pakistani peacekeepers, killing of, 60–1
peace conferences, 64, 133, 168, 199
    see also reconciliation conferences
piracy, 1, 14, 107, 109, 142–65; 'catch
    and release' policy, 159–60;
    economy of, 152–4; fear of pirates
    claiming asylum, 160–1; first trial
    case of, 160; hostages, killed in
    rescue, 162; investment structure
    of, 156–7; lack of laws to deal with,
    159–61; property boom linked
    to, 155; ransoms, 148, 152, 154
    (distribution of, 153); reduced in
    Somaliland, 164–5; relationship
    with radical Islam, 157–8; seen
    as *haraam* by UIC, 157; torture of
    hostages, 163–4; use of mother
    ships, 145; written rules of
    conduct, 157
poetry, 26–9
Portugal, 46
poverty, alleviation projects, 158
property boom linked to piracy, 155
psychiatrists, lack of, 130
Puntland, 9, 43, 50, 66, 109, 111, 137,
    160, 185, 200; naming of, 3, 18–19;
    piracy in, 153 *see also* Land of Punt

Qadiriya brotherhood, 75
Qaeda, al-, organization, 1, 4, 5, 13, 40,
    49, 70, 74, 77, 84, 86, 88, 96, 101,
    166, 170, 171, 173–4, 188
Qaran group, 136
Qasin, Maryam, 25
qat, 116, 121; addiction to, 155;
    banning of, 10, 78, 81 (effects of,
    82); importation of, 10; induces
    psychosis, 30; use of, 29–30

quiz on Islamic faith, 90
Quraysh tribe, 45

Raaghe, Ali Mohamud, 181, 188
Rahanweyn clan, 39
rap music, 28
rape, 58
Rathore, Dipendra, 163
reconciliation conferences, 8–9
refugees, 33, 113, 181; camps, 119, 121,
    173 (Dadaab camp, 188); from
    Mogadishu, 175; to Yemen, 187
regional implications of Somalia
    developments, 184–5
remittances of Somalis, 120 *see also*
    al-Barakat company
Rift Valley Fever, 119
Riyale, Dahir, 136
roads, building of, 128
Rodd, James Rennell, 7, 53
Rotberg, Robert, 106
Russia, 51

Salad, Omar, 58–9
Salihiya brotherhood, 75
Samatar, Abdi, 174
Samatar, Abdillahi Sa'iid, 154
Samatar, Said S., 68–9
Saudi Arabia: bans on livestock
    exports, 17, 118–19; export of
    camels to, 16; export of sea food
    to, 20
School of Oriental and African Studies
    (SOAS), 105
'Scramble for Africa', 46
seafaring tradition of Somalis, 14
security, 85; maintenance of, role of
    al-Shabaab in, 71–2, 111; role of UIC
    in, 80–2
security companies, in ship
    protection, 143
segregation, of boys and girls, 73
Seychelles, prosecution of pirates, 161
Shabaab, al-, organization, 5, 23, 27–8,

33, 39, 40, 61, 66, 70, 71–3, 74, 85–96, 110, 123, 137, 172–3, 173–4, 177, 180, 181, 183, 184, 187, 189–90; links with al-Qaeda, 5; on US terrorist list, 86; recruiting by, 118, 191; support for, 179

Shakul, Mohamed Ibrahim, 192, 193

shalwar kameez, wearing of, 73

sharia courts, 4, 9, 41–2, 66, 79, 82, 170; relationship with clans, 80

sharia law, 75, 86; punishments, 10, 72, 79, 81, 91

Sharmarke, Omar Abdirashid Ali, 52, 54, 65, 164, 175–6

Shihri, Saeed al, 188

Shire, Barre Aden, 84

Siad Barre, Mohamed, 8, 11–12, 19, 28, 32, 38, 41, 43, 54, 76, 135; fall of, 44, 56, 77, 79, 85, 118; personality cult of, 41

Silanyo, Ahmed, 131, 136–7, 140

Sirius Star, hijacking of, 146–8

slaves, trading of, 46

socialism, 12; 'scientific', 41

Somali language, given written form, 12, 54

Somali National Security Agency, 178

Somali National Movement (SNM), 41, 43, 55–6

Somali Patriotic Movement (SPM), 56

Somali Salvation Democratic Front (SSDF), 41, 56

Somali schoolchildren in England, 1

Somali Youth Club, 51–2

Somali Youth League, 52

Somalia: apocalyptic accounts of, 107; as cockpit of Africa, 53; divided into mini-states, 34; history of, 44–70 (alternative authority period, 66–70; civil war, 56–60; colonial, 46–51; dictatorship, 54–6; independence, 51–4; intervention, 60–3; pre-colonial, 45–6; virtual government, 64–5); Italian colony of, 12; name of territory, 3; national flag of, 31; Republic announced, 52 *see also* Greater Somalia

Somalia Italiana, 49, 50, 51–2, 132

Somaliland, 9, 12, 31, 40, 43, 44, 49–50, 71, 102, 109, 111, 131–2, 167–8, 179, 185, 195, 198–9, 200; combating of piracy in, 164–5; name of territory, 3; recognition of, needed, 131; stability of, 13 *see also* British Protectorate of Somaliland

songs culture, 7

South Korean ships, treatment of, 157

Spanish ships, fishing in Somali waters, 20

state failure, perceived as security threat, 106

statehood: new model of, 4; paradigms of, 3

stateless Somalis, 98

stoning to death, 94

Sufism: brotherhoods, 74–5; desecration of graves of saints, 78

suicide bombings, 27, 66, 84, 86, 89, 96, 101–2, 174, 191

Supreme Revolutionary Council, 54

taxation, 82, 114, 193, 194

tea shops, 29

telecommunications, 119–25

Transitional Federal Government, 199

Triangle of Death, 59

tribalism, 54

trust, basis of business dealings, 116

Turabi, Hassan al-, 78

Turkey, 47–8

Turki, Hassan, 78

Uganda, 136, 176, 184–5; al-Shabaab killings in, 102

Union of Islamic Courts (UIC), 4–5, 9, 33, 41–2, 44, 51, 77, 78, 79–85, 157–8, 170, 172, 174, 179, 186, 195,

198; perceived as threat, 103–4; reduce problem of piracy, 164–5

Union of Soviet Socialist Republics (USSR), 41, 54; changes support policy, 55

UNITAF mission, 60

United Kingdom (UK), 7; blamed for transfer of Ogaden, 51; policy in Somalia, 46–51, 132, 138, 179, 189, 200; Somali community in, 101; use of aerial bombing, 48

United Nations (UN), 64, 113, 167, 177, 186; agencies, relation to aid exploitation, 183; arms embargo against Somalia, 155–6; declaration of famine, 2, 182–3; estimates of Somali refugees, 33; forces in Somalia, 6; peacekeeping operations, 60–3; piracy monitoring group, 154; report on al-Shabaab activities, 95; report on insecurity in Somalia, 199; report on Somali Islamism, 191; Seychelles piracy agreement, 161; transmission of funds to Somalia, 121; trusteeship in Somalia, 50, 51

UN Convention on the Law of the Sea, 159

UN Security Council, 60; report on food aid, 183; report on security, 175

UN World Food Programme (WFP), 63, 145, 183

United Somali Congress (USC), 41, 56

United States of America (USA), 1, 3, 38, 43, 49, 51, 79, 83, 84, 88, 142, 174, 182, 186, 190; air strikes against Islamist suspects, 172; arms shipments to African Union, 178; arms shipments to Somalia, 177; as global policeman, 62; bombing of embassies of, 168; bombing of Somalia, 84, 180;

drone attacks by, 179; forces of (aggressive behaviour of, 61; landing in Somalia, 60); National Security Strategy, 106, 169–70; perceived threats to, 100; policy on Ethiopia, 4, 180; policy on Somalia, 5–6, 108, 132, 138, 168–71, 177–8, 179, 198, 200; policy on UIC, 66; Somali communities in, 99–101

Unity of Democrats (UDUB), 135

UNOSOM mission, 60, 62, 63, 64

UNOSOM II mission, 60

Uwah, a Somali woman, 114

Vaux, Tony, 59

veiling *see* women, veiling of

Walls, Michael, 23, 140

'War on Terror', 51, 168–71, 181, 186, 190; Somalia's inclusion in, 197

warlords, 77, 79, 80, 82, 170

water resources, access to, 112

Watson, Murray, 57

Wikileaks, 175

women: dress of, 71; nicknames of, 28; nomadic, 23–5; rights of, 76; veiling of, 10, 71, 73, 78, 81, 94, 126

World Cup final bombings, 66

World Health Organization (WHO), 25

xawilaad money system, 119

xeer conflict resolution system, 40, 115, 120

Yassin, Ali Sheikh, 93

Yemen, 96–7, 166, 187–8; availability of weapons from, 156

Yusuf, Abdullahi, 65, 176

Zawahiri, Ayman al-, 84

Zeila town, 46

Zenawi, Meles, 83

About Zed Books

Zed Books is a critical and dynamic publisher, committed to increasing awareness of important international issues and to promoting diversity, alternative voices and progressive social change. We publish on politics, development, gender, the environment and economics for a global audience of students, academics, activists and general readers. Run as a co-operative, Zed Books aims to operate in an ethical and environmentally sustainable way.

Find out more at:

www.zedbooks.co.uk

For up-to-date news, articles, reviews and events information visit:

http://zed-books.blogspot.com

To subscribe to the monthly Zed Books e-newsletter, send an email headed 'subscribe' to:

marketing@zedbooks.net

We can also be found on **Facebook**, **ZNet**, **Twitter** and **Library Thing**.